ONE TECH AT A TIME

ONE TECH AT A TIME

The Everyday Guide to All Things Digital in the Workplace

JORDI GUIU PONT

Superpowered by Artificial Intelligence

Contents

Who I Am and Why I Wrote This Book

Born in 1984 in Barcelona, I was ushered into a world where computers were primarily confined to bank offices, teenagers grooved to music on cassettes, and only three TV channels existed where I lived.

Sounds decidedly non-digital, doesn't it? I was rooted in an entirely analog world. Fortunately, my father's fascination with computers and technology ensured that I was introduced to this realm from a tender age.

While the late eighties saw most households equipped with just basic electronics like TVs and radios, our home was an exception. We experimented with rudimentary computers—ones operated with cassette tapes and floppy disks—that my father procured out of sheer hobbyist passion.

As the nineties dawned, we rode the home computer revolution wave: experiencing our first color screens, marveling at our initial CD-ROM reader (which cost a staggering 300 euros at the time), witnessing the evolution of inkjet printers, and much more.

If you're in your late 30s or older, this narrative might evoke a sense of nostalgia, reminding you of your initial forays into the beginning of the digital age. And for the younger readers? Though this might sound like an alien epoch, it encapsulates the technological reality many of us experienced during our formative years. For me, this period was nothing short of magical, nurturing an enduring passion for technology, computing, and later, the internet. This enthusiasm drove me professionally, compelling me to stay abreast of technological innovations. My journey has seen me work in the eCommerce and tech sectors, intertwining technology with my professional persona.

Today, as information technologies pervade every facet of our lives, I frequently find myself enthusiastically demystifying tech concepts for friends and family. Despite the ubiquity of smartphones and digital workplace tools, a significant number of people I know grapple with grasping the basics of IT, turning our conversations into seemingly foreign dialogues.

Recognizing this disconnect, I've felt over the last few years a growing urge to share with close friends and family the fundamental concepts of information technologies. My aim this time? To assist not just my close ones, but by creating this book, to help countless others, I hope thousands, in navigating our digitally-transforming world and catching up with its rapid pace.

You can learn more about me and my work at jordiguiu.com or onetechatatime.com

Who Is This Book For

Has this ever happened to you?

Ever sat in a meeting nodding along, pretending to understand when someone mentioned "ERP" or other strange techie terms? Or maybe your bank emailed you a warning about "phishing" and you wondered if it had something to do with fish?

Heard about the wonders of artificial intelligence on the radio, only to have an internal moment of panic about what it means for the future of jobs? Or, have a family member working in a tech role that might as well be wizardry for all you understand?

You're not alone. The rapid pace of digital transformation happening at work and everywhere can make many of us feel left behind. And guess what? Ignoring it doesn't make it go away. This world of tech, from the mysterious acronyms to the groundbreaking innovations, is shaping our lives and jobs every day.

If any of these scenarios felt all too familiar, then it's time for a change. This book is your guide to catching up, to understanding the digital transformation at work without the jargon and confusion.

Let's make sure the digital environment, the language and tools in the workplace are something you navigate with confidence, not apprehension.

I would like you to gain this confidence in a way you too can leverage digital technology to become a better version of yourself in your current job or your future aspirations.

Would you like to hear a great example of how that is possible? Well, the creation of this book serves as a prime illustration. By leveraging the capabilities of artificial intelligence, specifically a language model like ChatGPT, I was able to transform my insights and experiences into a comprehensive guide in a record time of about 4 weeks—a timeframe that would have been tenfold longer had I not utilized these tools. This collaboration between human expertise and AI efficiency embodies the incredible advancements shaping the 2020s—the decade of AI.

I want this book to be a source of empowerment for you, just as AI has empowered me to become an author. Technology isn't just for the tech-savvy; it's for everyone. It's here to augment our abilities, broaden our horizons, and yes, even help us understand and keep up with the digital transformation.

Let's embark on this journey together. By the end of it, my hope is that you'll not only understand the digital workplace but also be inspired to leverage technology in ways that enhance your personal and professional life.

What You Will Find in This Book

The pages ahead offer a guide crafted specifically for readers like you. It's clear that not everyone is naturally inclined towards technology, and that's okay.

This book is designed to simplify, yet thoroughly explain, the essential information technology concepts encountered in daily professional life across various sectors, tech and non-tech alike. Armed with this knowledge, you'll navigate work environments with ease, especially when these tech concepts pop up in discussions or tasks.

For the fortunate, intellectually active retirees out there, this book serves as an insightful crash course on the digital transformation sweeping society. Your curiosity will be well-served!

Structured over 10 modules, this book dives into thematic areas of information technology and common organizational functions within numerous companies.

These modules collectively dissect 75 concepts, each presented in a bite-sized chapter format. You can digest each of these chapters in under a minute, complete with practical examples, potential challenges, and a look into the concept's future trajectory.

Use this book as a comprehensive guide, reading it cover to cover for a broad overview, or cherry-pick specific chapters that pique your interest. Either way, the simple, jargon-free language ensures a smooth read, even for those without a tech background. And if a particular topic sparks your curiosity for a deeper dive, there's always a vast digital ocean of information online.

Whether you're looking to boost your workplace confidence, venture into new professional territories, or simply satiate personal curiosity, I sincerely hope this book brings you joy and insight.

Starting this journey, you're taking a pivotal step towards your personal digital transformation. Let's ensure you stay ahead of the curve in 2024 and beyond!

Are you ready?

Book Modules

Our journey through 2023 edition:

Module 1 - Information Technologies Foundations.
Start with the ABC.

Module 2 - Main Information Technologies.
The Big Things since you went to school.

Module 3 - Software development.
Lighting the blackhole of developers' universes.

Module 4 - Artificial Intelligence.
The next (now!) Big Thing.

Module 5 - Data Analysis and Data Science.
What are these data driven decisions?

Module 6 - Cybersecutiry.
Be prepared. Stay safe.

Module 7 - Digital Marketing.
It's not just social media.

Module 8 - Enterprise tools.
The backstage of businesses.

Module 9 - Fintech.
Money in the age of technology.

Module 10 - Other Concepts.
Last bits and bytes.

Module 1 - Information Technologies Foundations. Start with the ABC.

In this module we are going to be grasping the very basics, like the difference between hardware and software or understanding what a server does.

As we get those, we will be delving into topics like algorithms, databases, and cloud computing to reveal the sophisticated machinery operating behind the user-friendly interfaces we see in our phone or computer..

Humans are part of the chapter as well, so we will understand what software developers do.

In essence, this module lays the groundwork for understanding the expansive world of Information Technologies. It serves as a primer or the foundation to be able to go through our journey.

If you feel comfortable with the basics already, feel free to skip this module and just start your journey in module 2 that goes through main information technologies.

Otherwise, let's dive into it!

Concept 1: Software
The Invisible Magic Powering Your Digital Life

You know that frustrating moment when you're yelling at your computer because it refuses to cooperate? "Why won't you work, you blasted machine?!" Spoiler alert: It's not usually the computer's fault. More often, it's about the software inside. So, what is software? Let's dive in

Software is the term used to group any type of program or application that works on a digital device. It contains all the instructions and data that direct a computer to perform specific tasks. Think of it as the brain behind the operation, guiding hardware (like your phone or computer) to execute particular functions and tasks, be it sending emails, playing a game, or running complex simulations. Software can be anywhere—on your devices, in the cloud, and embedded in various technologies. Software is created by writing code in any of the programming languages that exist today.

Practical Examples

Microsoft Word or Google Docs: The trusty tool we all somehow have a love-hate relationship with. This software can be installed on your computer (desktop) or cloud based.

Instagram: Double-tap if you've ever lost yourself in the endless scroll of this social media app. Instagram it's a complex piece of software built by hundreds of developers.

Zoom: Zoom facilitates video conferencing by using the camera and microphone on any device. It's a cross-platform software that works on smartphones, tablets and computers.

Potential Pitfalls

Not all software is created equal. Some software might be ridden with bugs, causing it to malfunction or crash frequently. Also, using outdated software can leave you vulnerable to security threats, as it might not be equipped with the latest security features. And let's not forget the classic trap of freeware which, although free, might be limited in features, nudging you towards a paid version for full functionality. Navigating through the vast ocean of software choices requires a discerning eye, ensuring you pick ones that are secure, reliable, and suited to your needs.

Emerging Trends and Future Outlook

A glimpse into the future teases an even more software-dominated landscape, where Artificial Intelligence (AI) and Machine Learning (ML) take the driver's seat, steering software towards uncharted territories of possibilities.

Imagine software that learns from you, adapting and personalizing itself to cater to your preferences and needs. Also, with the rise of the Internet of Things (IoT), software will not only reside in our computers and phones but will be embedded in everyday objects—fridges, mirrors, and even clothing. So, buckle up! The software journey ahead is bound to be an exciting, albeit twisty, ride through innovations and transformations in every aspect of our lifes.

Concept 2: Hardware

The Tangible Backbone of the Digital Age

Picture your computer without its familiar casing, keyboard, or screen. What you'd uncover is a complex world of circuits, chips, and components: the hardware. While software is the soul, giving life to our devices, hardware is the body, the tangible parts you can touch, see, and often hear as they whir and click in operation.

Hardware refers to the physical components of a computer or any electronic system. This includes the central processing unit (CPU), memory (RAM), storage devices like hard drives, and input/output devices such as keyboards, mouse, and monitors. While they might seem just metal and plastic, their intricate designs and functionalities form the foundation upon which all software runs as hardware components perform all basic operations.

Practical Examples

Smartphones: Our pocket-sized powerhouse that allows us to communicate, browse, work, and entertain ourselves, are complex and highly miniaturized hardware devices.

Printers: Translating our digital documents into physical copies, are built by electro-mechanical components and managed by a software built-in their circuits.

Fitness Trackers: Monitoring our physical activities, health stats, and sleep patterns, these devices contain not only the screen and CPU (central brain) but also many sensors.

Potential Pitfalls

The majestic concert of hardware isn't always pitch-perfect. Hardware can wear out, break down, or become obsolete, especially in the rapidly evolving tech landscape. Being predominantly physical, hardware is susceptible to damage – a spill on the laptop or a drop can disrupt its functionality. Upgrades can be costly and sometimes, certain pieces of hardware may not be compatible with new software versions, restricting access to updated features and functionalities.

Emerging Trends and Future Outlook

Gazing into the horizon, we see hardware becoming increasingly compact yet more powerful. The proliferation of wearable technology and smart homes points towards a future where hardware seamlessly blends into our environment and daily routines.

Imagine glasses that overlay digital information onto the real world, or biosensors embedded in our clothes, monitoring and reporting our health data in real-time. Hardware is set to become not just tools we use but extensions of our physical selves, ever-present, and quietly enhancing our lives.

Concept 3: Databases

The Silent Custodians of Digital Memories and Information

Ever wondered where your saved contacts, the products of an online store, or even the scores of your favorite games are stored? It's not just floating around in cyberspace. All this information resides in databases. Databases are the digital vaults that store, organize, and manage vast amounts of data, ensuring it's both accessible and secure whenever needed.

Zooming in technically, a database is a structured collection of interrelated data, managed and stored electronically. It is designed to efficiently handle data retrieval and storage operations using software known as a Database Management System (DBMS). Relational databases, like SQL, store data in tables, while NoSQL databases, such as MongoDB, might use document-based structures, depending on the nature and variety of the data.

Practical Examples

Online Retail: Every product detail, customer review, or order history on sites like Amazon or eBay is stored in a database. When you search for a product, you're querying the database to fetch and display the relevant results.

Banking Systems: Your bank keeps track of your balances, transaction histories, and personal details using intricate database systems. This ensures that every deposit, withdrawal, or transfer is accurately recorded and retrievable.

Social Media: Platforms like Facebook or Twitter store every post, comment, like, or share in databases. These databases manage billions of users' data, making your memories and interactions readily available whenever you log in.

Potential Pitfalls

While databases have revolutionized data management, they are not without their hitches. Security concerns, such as unauthorized access and data breaches, cast a looming shadow over databases, especially those storing sensitive information. Additionally, managing and maintaining a database requires specialized skills and knowledge. The complexity escalates with the size of the database, and ensuring that data is accurate, consistent, and available when needed becomes a meticulous task.

Emerging Trends and Future Outlook

The future of databases is shaped by the ever-growing volume of data. With the Internet of Things (IoT) and smart devices proliferating, there's an increasing demand for real-time databases that can handle vast streams of live data. Technologies like edge computing are pushing databases closer to the source of data generation, allowing for faster processing. The rise of decentralized databases, powered by blockchain technology, is set to revolutionize data storage by ensuring transparency and eliminating single points of failure. Ethical considerations are paramount, especially with concerns over data privacy and ownership. As databases grow smarter, there's a pressing need to ensure they're built and used responsibly.

Chapter 4: Algorithm

The Digital Recipes Found Everywhere Around Us

From a thermostat deciding when to heat your room, a coffee machine brewing your morning drink, to your favorite streaming platform suggesting the next movie: all these actions rely on algorithms. Think of them as digital recipes, guiding devices and platforms step-by-step to produce the desired result.

Diving a bit deeper, we will find algorithms written in any piece of software code. An algorithm is a finite set of well-defined instructions to address a specific problem or task. These aren't just confined to computers; you'll find algorithms at work in everyday appliances, mobile apps, and even in systems managing traffic lights in cities. They ensure tasks are executed in the most efficient way, taking into account the provided data and desired outcome.

Practical Examples

Search Engines: Google and other search engines use intricate algorithms to sift through billions of web pages, ranking and delivering the most pertinent results in a flash.

Navigation Apps: Google Maps algorithms analyze multiple routes, weighing factors like current traffic conditions and road quality, to suggest the optimal path to your destination.

E-commerce Recommendations: Algorithms in online shopping sites process your browsing habits, previous purchases, and trends among similar users to handpick items you might find interesting.

Potential Pitfalls

Algorithms, while indispensable and smart, are not immune to challenges. They can inadvertently perpetuate biases if the data they are trained on contains biases—leading to skewed or unfair outcomes. Also, while algorithms can process data at lightning speeds, they lack the ability to understand context or apply common sense in unforeseen situations. Consequently, results or decisions produced by them might sometimes miss the mark or lack nuanced understanding.

Trends and Future Outlook

Because of the rise of Artificial Intelligence (AI), the algorithmic world is rapidly expanding into territories where ethical, fair, and unbiased decision-making is paramount. Innovations are leaning towards creating algorithms that are not just technically proficient but also ethically sound and transparent. Explainable AI, which refers to making algorithms transparent and understandable to humans, is gaining traction to ensure that decisions made by machines can be scrutinized and validated by humans. Further, we're witnessing an era where quantum algorithms are on the horizon, promising capabilities that could potentially solve complex problems beyond the reach of classical algorithms in the fields of genetics, space exploration and more.

Chapter 5: Servers

The Digital Librarians Organizing and Sharing the Web's Content

You've probably heard about websites being "down" or "the server crashed." But what exactly is a server? Think of a server as a vast digital librarian. Just as a librarian organizes and lends out books, a server stores, manages, and delivers digital content like websites, emails, and files to your computer or smartphone upon request.

Technically speaking, a server is a specialized computer or software system designed to process requests and deliver data to another computer over a local network or the internet. They differ from your typical desktop computers in their functionality, size, and purpose. Servers handle vast amounts of data, ensure multiple users can access content simultaneously, and prioritize security and reliability.

Practical Examples

Website Hosting: Every website you visit daily is stored on servers. When you type in the website's address or click on a link, the server presents the requested page to your browser.

Email Services: Providers like Gmail or Outlook have servers specifically for email. These store your messages and ensure they're sent, received and keep them accessible on any device.

Online Gaming: Popular games like Fortnite or Minecraft use servers to connect players from around the globe, ensuring smooth gameplay, syncing player actions, and updating game data in real-time.

Potential Pitfalls

Servers, despite being robust, are not infallible. They can be susceptible to overloads if too many requests are sent simultaneously, leading to slowdowns or even temporary unavailability—a scenario known as server downtime. Moreover, they can be targets for cyber-attacks like DDoS attacks that disrupt normal traffic and services. Properly maintaining, securing, and updating servers is crucial to ensure uninterrupted, secure services to users.

Emerging Trends and Future Outlook

The world of servers is not static; it's evolving rapidly in response to the ever-growing digital demands of businesses and consumers. Edge computing, for instance, is a trend pushing server resources closer to the user, allowing for faster response times, especially crucial for applications like self-driving cars or augmented reality. Moreover, green computing initiatives are driving the development of servers that consume less power, reducing environmental impacts. As more businesses transition to the cloud, hybrid server solutions that combine on-premises infrastructure with cloud resources are becoming popular, providing flexibility and scalability. But as servers grow more interconnected and essential, there's an increased emphasis on security. There's a pressing need to guard against cyber threats, emphasizing the development of robust server security measures. Reflecting ethically, it's essential for companies to ensure data integrity and user privacy, given the significant amount of personal and sensitive data servers often hold.

Chapter 6: Cloud Computing

The Invisible Warehouse Storing the Digital World

Have you ever wondered where your emails, photos, or documents go when you save them "to the cloud"? Imagine an invisible, vast digital warehouse, always available, and accessible from anywhere. That's the essence of cloud computing.

In technical terms, cloud computing refers to the delivery of various services over the internet, such as storage, databases, software, and more. Instead of saving files on a personal computer or server, you save them on a remote database. These databases, or "clouds," can store vast amounts of information, and the beauty is that they're maintained by third parties, ensuring smooth operation and instant scalability.

Real-world Examples

File Storage: Platforms like Google Drive, Dropbox, or iCloud allow users to store photos, documents, and videos in the cloud, making them accessible from any device.

Software on Demand: Adobe Creative Cloud or Microsoft 365 offer software applications directly from the cloud, eliminating the need for physical installations.

Streaming Services: Netflix, Spotify, and YouTube stream vast amounts of data from the cloud, allowing for instant access to movies, music, and videos.

Potential Pitfalls

With great cloud power comes great responsibility! The centralized nature of cloud computing can pose risks like data breaches and loss if not managed and secured meticulously. Moreover, reliable internet connectivity is pivotal; without it, accessing the cloud might become a challenge.

Additionally, concerns about data privacy, compliance with regional data protection laws, and ensuring that the cloud service providers implement robust security protocols are paramount.

Emerging Trends and Future Outlook

Cloud computing's future holds exciting prospects. One trend is multi-cloud strategies, where businesses use multiple cloud service providers, tapping into each strengths.

Ethically, as cloud usage grows, so does the importance of security and data sovereignty. With data spread globally, ensuring it's protected and compliant with local regulations becomes paramount in an era of geo-political instability.

Chapter 7: Software Developer

The Digital Architects Crafting Our Digital Experience

Whenever you use an app, visit a website, or play a game, you're interacting with the result of a program (or code) written by software developers. Think of them as the architects and builders of the digital realm, crafting every detail to ensure you have a seamless experience.

At the heart, a software developer is a professional responsible for designing, coding, and testing software applications. They use programming languages, frameworks, and tools to build software that meets user needs or solves specific problems. Whether it's a mobile app, desktop software, or a website, developers are behind the scenes, making the magic happen thanks to written code executed by our devices.

Practical Examples

Web Development: Web developers specialize in building and maintaining websites and web applications. They work on everything from simple informational sites to complex web-based applications, e-commerce platforms, and social networking sites. This involves understanding both front-end (user interface and experience) and back-end (server, database, and application) development.

Mobile Development: Mobile developers are focused on creating applications for mobile devices like smartphones and tablets. They need to account for different operating systems like iOS and Android, ensuring optimal performance and user experience on various devices.

Potential Pitfalls

While developers weave the digital world, they may face numerous challenges. One is staying updated with the ever-evolving tech, languages, and tools, ensuring their skills remain relevant and potent. Balancing functionality and user-friendliness in a product, managing time and resources efficiently, and dealing with bugs and errors in code are constant hurdles that developers leap over during their digital creation journey.

Emerging Trends and Future Outlook

The world of software development is in perpetual motion. DevOps, a fusion of development and operations, emphasizes collaboration, automation, and continuous delivery.

Low-code and no-code platforms are emerging, enabling even non-developers to create applications.

On the ethical front, there's increasing emphasis on transparent coding practices, data protection, and considerations about how software can impact society, from misinformation propagation to potential job displacement.

Module 1 Closing

Embarking on the journey through Module 1, the exploration of foundational technological elements, we uncovered not merely their functional attributes but their roles as pivotal entities within our digital world. Let's recap them:

Unified Digital Frameworks: Software unfolds not merely as coded programs but as the backbone, connecting and orchestrating various technological entities into a unified, functional digital ecosystem.

Tangible Tech Foundations: Hardware isn't simply physical tech components but the tangible foundation that houses, enables, and powers the digital experiences.

Data, the Quiet Custodian: Databases are crucial custodians and organizers of data, ensuring information is not only securely stored but accessible to be used when needed.

Coded Decision Making: Algorithms transcend mere logic codes, emerging as the brains behind digital operations, making calculated decisions, predicting patterns, and automating processes with precision and intelligence.

Digitally Interconnected: Servers act not merely as data distributors but as the interconnected web that seamlessly binds different digital facets together, ensuring information and services are accessible whenever and wherever needed.

Boundless Digital Expansion: Cloud Computing provides more than remote servers—it offers boundless opportunities for scalability, flexibility, and innovative digital expansion without the physical confines of traditional tech infrastructure.

Beyond Coding: Developers are not just coders but architects of the digital world, crafting the landscapes, experiences, and functionalities that populate and power our digital interactions and dependencies.

Module 2 - Main Information Technologies. The big things since you went to school.

Welcome to "Main Information Technologies: The Big Things Since You Went to School." This module journeys through the transformative tech shifts that have reshaped our world since the days of chalkboards and overhead projectors.

You may have heard of terms like Artificial Intelligence, Blockchain, or even the mysterious Web3. But what do they mean? How have they influenced industries, businesses, and our daily lives?

This module offers a guide through the major tech milestones of recent years. Dive in and rediscover the digital world as we know it today.

Chapter 8: Ecommerce platforms

The new shopping malls and street markets.

Your local store has gone global. Remember weekend shopping sprees? It seems now you prefer the convenience of anytime, without stepping out of your home, just click and receive it. Ecommerce platforms are digital marketplaces, bridging buyers and sellers in the vast online universe.

Going technical, ecommerce platforms are more than just websites. They combine catalog management, shopping carts, payment gateways, and customer relationship tools. Sophisticated systems like Shopify, WooCommerce, or Magento can handle everything from product display to sales analytics, making global commerce a breeze.

Practical Examples

Amazon: We all know it, we all use it. Starting off as a humble bookstore, Amazon has metamorphosed into an ecommerce behemoth, proving the limitless potential of online selling.

Etsy: A unique touch in the digital age. Catering to handmade, vintage, and craft-based products, Etsy stands as a testament to the fact that niche, community-based markets can not only survive but thrive in the online sphere.

Alibaba: It's not just about individual buyers. Alibaba shows how businesses can connect, with manufacturers meeting retailers, making global trade more seamless than ever.

Potential Pitfalls

Ecommerce platforms, despite providing ease and global market access, can present challenges. Ensuring cybersecurity to protect customer data, managing high-quality customer service in a virtual space, and staying competitive in a crowded digital market are continual hurdles.

Additionally, maintaining a robust, user-friendly interface and managing logistical aspects like shipping and returns are critical to ensuring customer satisfaction and loyalty.

Emerging Trends and Future Outlook

Ecommerce isn't just about buying and selling anymore; it's about experiences. Personalized shopping journeys using AI, augmented reality for a virtual "try-before-you-buy", and social commerce integrating shopping with social media interactions are redefining retail.

On the horizon? A world where your shopping experience is as unique as you are, provided ethical considerations, especially around data privacy, are maintained. This digital boom also emphasizes the importance of data privacy and ethical business practices in the online realm.

Chapter 9: Software as a Service (SaaS)

Beyond Installations: Software in the Cloud Era

We've all been there: too many apps, too little space on our devices. Then along comes SaaS, with a brilliant proposition: Why not just rent the software instead of buying and installing it? Suddenly, you have access to the software you need, right from your web browser, without using up precious storage space.

Software as a Service, or SaaS, is a cloud-computing approach to accessing software. Instead of purchasing, downloading, and installing applications directly to your device, SaaS offers access to software directly via the internet, typically through a subscription model. From graphic design platforms to customer relationship management tools, SaaS platforms provide flexibility, scalability, and accessibility, enabling users to access sophisticated tools without hefty upfront costs or hardware requirements.

Practical Examples

Google Workspace (formerly G Suite) - Tools like Gmail, Docs, and Drive, accessible from anywhere, making collaboration seamless.

Salesforce - A leading customer relationship management tool that businesses use to track sales, customer interactions, and more.

Adobe Creative Cloud - Instead of buying standalone Adobe software, users can subscribe and get access to a suite of creative tools.

Potential Pitfalls

While SaaS offers immense advantages, it does bring challenges like ensuring consistent internet connectivity for unhindered access, managing subscription costs, and ensuring that chosen platforms are compliant with regional data protection regulations. Businesses often grapple with integrating different SaaS solutions and ensuring that their teams are adeptly trained to maximize the functionalities of these platforms. Data security and ensuring privacy compliance are also pivotal in the SaaS realm.

Emerging Trends and Future Outlook

The SaaS landscape is bustling with innovations. AI-driven automation, vertical SaaS tailored for specific industries, and micro-SaaS catering to niche markets are growing trends. As more businesses transition online, the demand for industry-specific solutions rises.

On the horizon? A landscape where businesses, regardless of size, have access to tailored software solutions that cater to their unique needs, ensuring they remain agile and competitive, while ethically balancing data security and privacy concerns.

Chapter 10 - Artificial Intelligence (AI)
Machines with Minds: The Future of computers

"Alexa, write a section on AI for my upcoming book." If only AI was advanced enough to craft full sections of a book with a mere voice command! Well, sort of. While we're not quite there yet, AI has undoubtedly seeped into our daily lives, quietly automating and enhancing various tasks and activities, including writing this book in two months instead of two years.

Artificial Intelligence, or AI, revolves around the creation of systems capable of performing tasks that would typically require human intelligence, such as understanding natural language, recognizing patterns, solving problems, writing and learning from experience. AI is not a futuristic robot; it's a computational tool that enhances the capability to process data, make decisions, and create user experiences that feel intuitively human, yet are powered by machines.

Practical Examples

Siri and Alexa: These virtual assistants utilize AI to comprehend voice commands, answer questions, play music, or manage other smart devices in your home.

Netflix Recommendations: Ever wondered how Netflix suggests movies you end up loving? It's AI in action, analyzing your watching habits and preferences.

Tesla's Autopilot: Tesla's AI-powered autopilot system can navigate highways, change lanes, and even park the car.

Potential Pitfalls

The road to intelligent machines isn't without its bumps. Issues such as data bias, where AI systems perpetuate existing biases in society, can lead to unequal and unfair outcomes. Additionally, concerns about job displacement due to automation and ethical questions about the role and decision-making capabilities of AI in critical aspects of human life (such as legal decisions or healthcare) are prevalent. Not to mention, managing the security of AI systems against potential malicious attacks is paramount.

Emerging Trends and Future Outlook

The future of AI points toward increased collaboration between humans and machines, enhancing our capabilities rather than replacing them. The rise of responsible AI, focused on ethical use, transparency, and fairness, is gaining traction, while the use of AI in augmenting reality, creating more personalized user experiences, and developing solutions for global challenges, such as climate change and health crises, is anticipated. Moreover, advancements in natural language processing will continue to refine how AI understands and interacts with human language, bridging the gap between machine operations and human communication.

Chapter 11: Augmented Reality (AR)

Blurring Boundaries: Melting Real and Virtual Views

Ever wished to add a layer of magic to your everyday world? AR does precisely that. It overlays digital information—like images, sounds, or other data—onto the real world around you, augmenting what you see through your eyes.

AR combines the use of cameras, sensors, and advanced algorithms to capture and process the real-world environment. As it determines the viewer's position and orientation, sophisticated software maps digital elements to that environment in real time. AR uses hardware as handheld displays or smart glasses to merge computer-generated objects with our reality. AR creates a dynamic and interactive experience, where digital entities can be anchored to physical locations or even respond to changes in the environment.

Practical Examples

Pokemon GO: This mobile game took the world by storm, sending players outdoors to "catch" virtual Pokémon that appear in real-world locations, thanks to AR.

IKEA Place: Before buying furniture, wouldn't it be great to visualize how it fits in your space? IKEA's AR app lets you do just that, placing life-sized virtual furniture in your room.

Snapchat Filters: Those fun and quirky face filters or world lenses that dance around your surroundings? That's AR at play, recognizing facial features or spaces to overlay dynamic digital elements.

Potential Pitfalls

While AR brings an immersive experience, it's not without challenges. Issues like technological limitations, privacy concerns, and digital distraction emerge. For instance, while using AR applications, personal and location data privacy must be safeguarded. Moreover, ensuring that immersive AR doesn't become a source of distraction, especially in scenarios like driving or walking on busy streets, is crucial. Lastly, technological hurdles like battery consumption and realistic rendering still pose considerable challenges to the current devices and services.

Emerging Trends and Future Outlook

As AR technologies mature, the boundary between our digital and physical worlds continues to blur. The future might see AR-enhanced classrooms where complex concepts come alive, or AR-powered tourism where historic events reenact right before our eyes. Additionally, with the advent of AR glasses, the information we need might be displayed seamlessly as we navigate our day. However, as this tech becomes more embedded in our lives, it's essential to tread the fine line between augmentation and intrusion, ensuring that our augmented experiences remain ethical and privacy-focused.

Chapter 12 - Virtual Reality (VR):

Beyond the Screen: Immersive Digital Dive-ins

Imagine stepping into a world where everything, from sights to sounds, is crafted digitally, immersing you in a reality separate from our own. That's the allure of VR. It's a simulated experience, sometimes similar to the real world and other times utterly fantastical.

Technically speaking, VR relies on headsets equipped with special lenses to produce lifelike visuals and acoustics that create a believable alternate world. Advanced VR systems might also offer tactile feedback, track hand movements, or even capture body motion, allowing users to interact naturally within these digital realms.

Practical Examples

Oculus Rift: A leading name in VR tech, Oculus Rift provides a full immersion experience, allowing users to step into their favorite games or explore faraway lands.

Google Earth VR: Ever wanted to fly over your hometown or visit an international landmark? Google Earth VR lets you traverse the globe virtually, exploring landscapes in a 3D format.

Virtual Real Estate Tours: Especially relevant in the age of remote work and travel restrictions, these tours let potential buyers or renters explore properties in-depth without being physically present.

Potential Pitfalls

Navigating through the enthralling universes of VR is not without its challenges. The technology can be cost-prohibitive for many, restricting access to its mesmerizing worlds. Then there's the concept of VR sickness, where the disparity between what users see and feel can cause discomfort or nausea. Additionally, ensuring that VR experiences are accessible and enjoyable for people with various disabilities poses a substantial developmental hurdle.

Emerging Trends and Future Outlook

The future of VR is a boundless expanse of possibilities. Beyond gaming and entertainment, VR is making headways into healthcare, offering therapeutic interventions and surgical training. In the realm of education, imagine learning about ancient civilizations, not from a textbook, but by virtually walking through an ancient city! Also, VR is poised to revolutionize remote work, providing immersive collaborative environments that transcend physical boundaries. Moreover, as VR technology becomes more affordable and accessible, it is likely to become a staple in our digital experiences, reshaping our recreational, professional, and social interactions.

Chapter 13: Internet of Things (IoT)
Connected everything Devices that Speak and Listen

Imagine a world where your coffee machine starts brewing just as your alarm rings, or your washing machine sends you a text when your laundry is done. This isn't science fiction; it's the Internet of Things (IoT), making everyday objects smarter and more connected.

IoT refers to the network of physical objects embedded with sensors, software, and other technologies to connect and exchange data with other devices and systems over the internet. Essentially, it allows objects to be sensed and controlled remotely, creating opportunities for more direct integration between the physical world and computer-based systems. From smart homes to connected healthcare, IoT propels us towards a future where our devices not only respond to our commands but also communicate, analyze, and act upon information amongst themselves.

Practical Examples

Smart Home Ecosystems: Google Nest allows users to control everything from heating to security cameras via voice or smartphone, transforming regular homes into smart homes.

Wearable Fitness Trackers: Devices like Fitbit not only track your steps but analyze your sleep, heart rate, and other health indicators, giving you insights into your wellness.

Smart Farming: Farmers use IoT devices to monitor soil moisture levels, enabling them to irrigate crops more efficiently and sustainably.

Potential Pitfalls

Diving into the IoT realm isn't without its potential snags. Privacy concerns are paramount – after all, if your devices are consistently communicating data, who is listening? Security is another mammoth concern since more connected devices mean more opportunities for cyber-attacks. Furthermore, the integration of so many different devices and technologies can lead to compatibility issues, requiring standardized protocols and extensive research and development.

Emerging Trends and Future Outlook

The horizon for IoT is vast and growing. From smart cities that manage waste in real-time to healthcare advancements with wearables that can predict potential health issues, the possibilities seem endless. However, as we integrate more of our lives with IoT, concerns about data privacy and security emerge. As we embrace a connected future, it becomes pivotal to establish robust safeguards, ensuring our devices serve us without compromising our privacy.

Chapter 14: 5G
A New Era of Connectivity

Remember the leap from slow-loading web pages on 3G to instant video streaming on 4G? Now, get ready for an even bigger jump. 5G promises to revolutionize how we connect, work, and play.

5G doesn't simply enhance the speed of internet connectivity; it's an entire network evolution. It brings accelerated data speeds, greater stability, and the capacity to connect a plethora of devices simultaneously. With reduced latency, 5G ensures that data sent between devices travels with minimal delay, crafting a seamlessly interactive digital experience and enabling technologies like autonomous driving, augmented reality, and IoT to thrive magnificently..

Practical Examples

Autonomous Vehicles: The lightning speed and minimal lag of 5G are critical for self-driving cars, where a fraction of a second can make the difference between a safe maneuver and a collision.

Telemedicine: 5G enables high-definition video calls and remote patient monitoring, ensuring doctors can perform real-time consultations without any delay, crucial for critical interventions.

Virtual Reality & Gaming: With 5G's high-speed connection, gamers can experience ultra-realistic multiplayer VR environments without any lags, redefining immersive gaming.

Potential Pitfalls

As we ride the lightning-fast waves of 5G, there are choppy seas ahead to navigate. The implementation of 5G demands colossal investment in infrastructure and poses compatibility issues with existing technologies. The need for extensive, dense networks of antennas could also mean urban areas benefit more, potentially widening the digital divide. And let's not forget, the dazzling speeds and connectivity also beckon for stringent security protocols to protect data integrity and privacy.

Emerging Trends and Future Outlook

5G's rollout is set to usher in a new era of innovation. It will be the backbone of smart cities, IoT devices, and innovations we've yet to dream up. However, the deployment of 5G also brings challenges, particularly around infrastructure costs and the concerns some have expressed about health impacts. As industries adapt to harness the full potential of 5G, they must also address these concerns, ensuring a future where technology benefits all while minimizing potential drawbacks.

Chapter 15: Blockchain

Trust Redefined in Bytes and Blocks

Heard of Bitcoin? While often associated with cryptocurrencies, there's a new technology behind them called "blockchain." This isn't just about digital money; it's about redefining trust in the digital age.

Peeling back the layers, a blockchain is a decentralized ledger of all transactions across a network. This means data is stored across multiple systems, and every time a transaction occurs, a record is created that's immutable and can't be altered without altering all subsequent records. It's a system built on transparency and incorruptibility.

Practical Examples

Cryptocurrencies: Bitcoin, the pioneer cryptocurrency, utilizes blockchain to track ownership and manage decentralized transactions without the need for a central bank.

Supply Chain: Companies like IBM employ blockchain for enhanced transparency and real-time tracking in their supply chain, ensuring authenticity and timely delivery of products.

Voting Systems: Emerging concepts suggest using blockchain to create tamper-proof voting systems, safeguarding the integrity of electoral processes by securely logging votes and ensuring transparency.

Potential Pitfalls

Traversing the blockchain pathway isn't devoid of stumbling blocks. The technology, though secure, faces challenges in scalability and energy consumption, especially in cryptocurrency mining. Its decentralized nature, while a strength, can be a double-edged sword, creating regulatory and compliance challenges. Plus, as industries consider adopting blockchain, the lack of standardization and skilled professionals becomes evident, presenting hurdles in practical implementation.

Emerging Trends and Future Outlook

Blockchain's potential extends far beyond its initial cryptocurrency application. We're beginning to see innovations in sectors like healthcare for patient record management, in finance for fraud prevention, and even in energy sectors for transparent trading.

As with all technologies, challenges exist. The energy consumption of blockchain, especially in cryptocurrency mining, and its scalability are concerns. Nonetheless, its promise to deliver a more transparent, trustworthy digital world is undeniably transformative.

Chapter 16: Decentralized finances (Defi)

When Your Finances Go Rogue

Decentralized finance, commonly referred to as DeFi, aims to recreate or enhance traditional financial systems using blockchain technology, primarily on the Ethereum network. By eliminating intermediaries like banks, DeFi offers more open, accessible, and transparent financial services.

In essence, DeFi leverages smart contracts, which are automated, self-executing contracts with the terms of the agreement written into lines of code. Its proponents claim that this system democratizes financial services, giving people direct control over their assets and transactions without relying on central authorities or intermediaries. In theory, It seeks to recreate and improve traditional financial systems (like lending and borrowing) in a decentralized manner, reducing the need for intermediaries and offering more access and control to the user.

Practical Examples

Uniswap: A decentralized exchange that allows users to swap various cryptocurrencies without the need for a centralized authority, enabling a peer-to-peer transaction system.

Compound: A DeFi lending protocol that allows users to earn interest on their cryptocurrencies by depositing them into one of several pools supported by the platform.

MakerDAO: It offers DAI, a stablecoin whose value is pegged to the US dollar, and it's backed by collateral in the form of cryptocurrency, making it decentralized.

Potential Pitfalls

While the land of DeFi promises financial autonomy, it's not a stroll without a stumble. The security is heavily dependent on smart contract integrity, and if there are bugs or vulnerabilities, your assets could be at risk. Furthermore, regulatory oversight is still playing catch-up with DeFi developments, meaning that user protection is not always guaranteed, paving a potentially risky pathway for the uninitiated.

Emerging Trends and Future Outlook

DeFi is curating a parallel financial universe that's scripting its own rules and instruments. Platforms are evolving with more secure and user-friendly interfaces, aiming to make DeFi more accessible to non-tech-savvy users. The emerging trend of "DeFi 2.0" is focusing on sustainability, aiming to solve issues related to scalability, interoperability, and compliance. As more traditional finance users peek into the DeFi world, a blend of decentralized and traditional finance – sometimes referred to as "CeDeFi" – is becoming a fascinating space to watch.

Chapter 17: Web3

Redefining the Web: A Decentralized Dawn of Online Interactions

If you've surfed the web, you've experienced Web1 (static web pages) and Web2 (interactive social media and e-commerce). But what about Web3? Is this the next evolution? This is what some web3 enthusiasts are saying (although I do have quite a few doubts about it).

Web3 represents a decentralized internet, a shift from server-based structures to blockchain-based systems. It's more than just websites—it's a whole ecosystem where in theory, as web3 proponents suggest, users have control over their data, identities, and transactions without relying heavily on intermediaries like big tech companies.

Practical Examples

Decentralized Finance (DeFi): Bypassing traditional banks, users can now borrow, lend, or earn interest on their assets directly on platforms like Compound or Uniswap.

Decentralized Social Networks: Platforms like Mastodon offer a user-controlled alternative to mainstream social media, where you own your data.

Decentralized Autonomous Organizations (DAOs): DAOs, like MolochDAO, allow members to make decisions and manage resources collectively without a central authority.

Potential Pitfalls

Navigating the waters of Web3 does come with its share of turbulence. Interoperability between different blockchain networks can be a technical challenge, and ensuring a seamless user experience amidst decentralized networks can be daunting. Moreover, while Web3 aims to democratize the internet, it is essential to ensure that it doesn't become a playground solely for the technically skilled, maintaining inclusivity for all users.

Emerging Trends and Future Outlook

Web3 proponents claim that Web3 is reshaping online power dynamics, giving more control to users and minimizing middlemen. As more decentralized applications (dApps) emerge, there's an optimistic view of a more open, transparent web. Yet, challenges exist, from technical hurdles, scalability issues, to public understanding and adoption. Web3 offers a vision of a peer-to-peer internet, but its mainstream future is still being crafted. I do think we really need to wait to see how Web3 materializes and expands and it's not written in stone that it will succeed.

Module 2 Closing

Module 2 took us on a journey through technologies that have been revolutionizing our online world. Our understanding of current technological realities has been expanded and enriched.

Let's summarize the key insights of the module:

Digitally Facilitated Commerce: Ecommerce Platforms serve not just as online stores but as facilitators of global digital commerce, bridging vendors and consumers across distances and niches.

Software, Unbound and Everywhere: SaaS isn't merely about software delivery but represents a shift towards accessibility, flexibility, and strategic value in how software is consumed and utilized across industries.

Empathetic and Intelligent Machines: Artificial Intelligence transcends what we understood to date that computers were capable of, encapsulating the ability to emulate human-like thinking, learning, and problem-solving.

Enhanced Reality: Augmented Reality is not just about overlaying digital elements but about enhancing our interaction and perception of the real world with digitally integrated information and experiences.

Immersive Digital Worlds: Virtual Reality offers more than immersive experiences but fully digital worlds that can mimic, augment, or diverge from our physical reality.

Interconnected Physicality: Internet of Things represents an interconnected physical world where data flows seamlessly between devices and systems.

Fast and Far-Reaching Connectivity: 5G is not merely a faster network but a facilitator for more connected, efficient, and innovative digital technologies and experiences.

Decentralized Trust: Blockchain represents a decentralized ledger that reshapes our concepts of trust, transparency, and security in digital transactions and data storage.

Digital Uniqueness: NFTs symbolize more than digital ownership, standing as unique, verifiable, and tradable assets in the digital space that bridge virtual and real-world value.

Decentralized Digital Future: Web3 is envisioned not merely as the next stage of the internet but as a decentralized, user-empowered digital future where data ownership and online interactions are reshaped.

In essence, this module was a deep dive into technologies that have been, and will continue to be, at the forefront of the next digital revolution.

Hopefully you are now familiar with them and ready to deep dive into how companies build our day to day Apps and solutions over these technologies.

Module 3 - Software development. Lighting the blackhole of developers' universes.

Software development, a field that seamlessly marries logic with creativity, and technicality with user-centricity to build the most innovative and delightful products of our times.

In this module we will see how Software development isn't confined to the intricate realms of front-end and back-end development but extends to embody a holistic approach where every click, swipe, and user interaction is meticulously crafted and engineered. It's an intricate dance between visual appeal and under-the-hood technical robustness, resulting in digital solutions that captivate and cater to end-users.

We'll also explore the pivotal role of UX and UI Design, user research and how the user, here, is not merely a recipient but a central figure around whom the entire digital experience is sculpted.

The module covers the main figures of software development teams as well as some technical concepts and common practices and methodologies in the industry.

Welcome to a journey through the art and science of developing software.

Chapter 18: Front-end Development
Unveiling the Digital Facade

Have you ever admired a website's beautiful design, smooth animations, or interactive buttons? That's the magic of front-end development, the art of crafting what you see and interact with directly on the web.

Diving a bit deeper, front-end development involves utilizing languages like HTML, CSS, and JavaScript. It's all about creating the visual aspects of a website or web application – everything that the user experiences directly. From the layout of a site to its colors, fonts, and responsive features that adjust to your device size, it's the front-end developer's job to ensure it all looks good and functions smoothly.

Practical Examples

Responsive Websites: Most websites you visit adjust their layout based on whether you're viewing on a phone, tablet, or desktop. This adaptability is a hallmark of good front-end development.

Interactive Web Apps: Think about tools like Canva, where you drag, drop, and design directly in your browser. The fluidity of such interactions is the result of skilled front-end work.

Web Games: Games like 2048 or browser-based quizzes that you might take on Facebook. They rely heavily on front-end technologies to create engaging user experiences.

Potential Pitfalls

However, the path of a front-end developer isn't without its bumps. Balancing aesthetic appeal with optimal performance can be a tightrope walk. Ensuring the website or application looks and functions consistently across various devices and browsers is another common challenge. Additionally, keeping pace with the ever-evolving tools, frameworks, and technologies in front-end development demands perpetual learning and adaptation.

Emerging Trends and Future Outlook

Front-end development is always evolving, with newer frameworks and libraries like React, Vue, and Angular leading the charge, enhancing the user experience and making the developer's job more efficient. The increasing importance of web accessibility ensures that sites are usable for all, regardless of physical or cognitive abilities.

Looking ahead, we can expect even more immersive web experiences, leveraging technologies like WebAssembly and augmented reality (AR) web integrations. As the web continues to evolve, the boundary between what we once thought of as "websites" and "applications" will blur even further.

Chapter 19: Back-End Development
The Hidden Workings Behind the Web Curtain

Ever wondered how when you click a button on a website, you're shown your personal profile, or how your shopping cart remembers items even after days? That's the realm of back-end development: the unseen powerhouse behind the scenes.

Back-end development is the backbone of any software application. We are talking about server-side development. It involves creating and maintaining the technology needed to power the components which enable the user-facing side of the website to exist. This development pertains to databases, servers, and applications, ensuring that all the gears behind the scenes are moving smoothly, ensuring a seamless user experience on the front end. Languages like Python, Java, Ruby, and frameworks such as Node.js and Django, facilitate the creation of the invisible machinery that ensures the site or app runs flawlessly, storing and retrieving data as needed.

Practical Examples

E-commerce Checkouts: When you proceed to checkout on sites like Amazon, the back-end processes ensure your order details, shipping information, and payment get processed securely and correctly.

Social Media Feeds: Your personalized feed on platforms like Instagram or Facebook is generated and fetched by sophisticated back-end systems, tailoring content specifically for you.

Cloud Storage: Services like Google Drive or Dropbox allow you to save, retrieve, and share files. It's the back-end systems that manage these vast amounts of data, ensuring files are available whenever you need them.

Potential Pitfalls

Despite their prowess, back-end developers grapple with challenges. Ensuring the server, application, and database communicate effectively with each other, managing and structuring vast amounts of data, and ensuring scalability and sustainability of back-end structures, especially as user numbers grow, can be complex and demanding tasks.

Emerging Trends and Future Outlook

The realm of back-end development is rapidly advancing with the rise of microservices and serverless computing. These innovations allow developers to build more scalable, efficient, and faster systems.

The increasing adoption of cloud services, with providers like AWS, Azure, and Google Cloud, is further changing how back-end infrastructures are designed and deployed. As we march into the future, expect even more robust and streamlined back-end solutions, especially with the growing emphasis on data security and user privacy.

Chapter 20: UX and UI Design.

Making Digital Interactions Delightful

Ever wondered why some apps just feel so good to use? It's like walking into a well-organized room where everything is in its right place. That's the magic of UX (User Experience) and UI (User Interface) Design.

Diving a bit deeper, UX (User Experience) Design is the process of understanding the user's needs and crafting a product that is user-friendly, intuitive, and meets the exact needs of the customer with simplicity and elegance. Meanwhile, UI (User Interface) Design, its close companion, involves creating aesthetically pleasing interfaces, ensuring that the visuals communicate well with the user's experience, guiding them gracefully through the digital world.

Practical Examples

Apple's iOS: Apple's operating systems, like iOS for iPhones, are hailed for their intuitive design. How you navigate applications, smooth transitions, consistent icons, and clear typography are all part of a well-thought-out UX and UI that's loved by hundreds of millions of users across the globe.

Airbnb: The ease with which you can browse listings, view and book a place on Airbnb's platform? That's UX at work, ensuring your journey from visitor to booker is seamless.

Accessibility Features: Enabling varied audiences to interact with technology, such as screen readers for visually impaired users or voice commands for differently-abled individuals, are brilliant manifestations of inclusive UX/UI design.

Potential Pitfalls

However, the journey of crafting user experiences and interfaces is sprinkled with challenges. Striking a balance between aesthetic appeal and functional simplicity, ensuring accessibility for a wide array of users, and staying attuned to ever-evolving user preferences and technological advancements can be akin to sailing through digital storms.

UX and UI design is still today a profession with plenty of opportunities ahead, so think about if you want to solve these challenges above.

Emerging Trends and Future Outlook

The future of UX/UI design is bright and inclusive. With advancements in AI, designs are becoming more personalized, predicting user needs even before they express them. Virtual Reality (VR) and Augmented Reality (AR) experiences, that offer more immersive and interactive user experiences, are also going to be an interesting field for UX and UI developments.

Voice UIs, like those in smart speakers, are making technology accessible for visually impaired users. Plus, the push for ethical design ensures digital products are built with user well-being in mind, reducing digital addiction and promoting healthier screen time.

Chapter 21: User Research
What Do Your Users Really Want?

Ever caught yourself thinking, why would anyone design it this way? User Research seeks to answer such questions, diving deep into understanding user behavior, needs, and motivations. Through a combination of observation and inquiry, it ensures that digital products are designed with the user's experience at the forefront.

Common user research techniques like surveys, interviews, usability testing, and ethnographic field studies provide invaluable insights. By employing these methods, companies get a direct line to users' thoughts, making certain that their products are not just appealing but intuitive and meaningful to the end user.

Practical Examples

Slack: Before becoming a household name in workplace communication, Slack's team conducted extensive user research. This helped them fine-tune features, ensuring that the platform met the communication needs of diverse teams effectively.

Netflix: The "because you watched" section on Netflix isn't conjured out of thin air but is meticulously crafted using insights derived from deep-diving into user viewing habits and preferences.

MailChimp: This email marketing tool is known for its ease of use. The MailChimp team relies heavily on User Research to understand the varying needs of businesses and marketers, ensuring that their tool remains accessible and effective.

Potential Pitfalls

However, User Research isn't always a sugary journey. Biased data, misinterpretation of user feedback, and over-reliance on quantitative or qualitative data without balancing the two can result in misdirected product development and misaligned user experiences.

Emerging Trends and Future Outlook

The future is about making User Research more inclusive and holistic. Companies are now focusing on "empathetic research", understanding the emotional and cultural nuances of users.

With the growth of VR and AR, researchers are exploring new ways to understand user behavior in these spaces. Additionally, there's a push to involve users in the research process actively, blurring the lines between designers and end-users for more collaborative solutions.

Chapter 22 - Information Architecture:
Organizing Digital Shelves

Ever felt lost on a website, not knowing where to click next? That's where Information Architecture (IA) steps in, ensuring you can find your way effortlessly. At its core, IA is the art and science of organizing and labeling data effectively to support usability. It's the digital equivalent of a librarian categorizing books in a library, ensuring you find what you need with ease.

Going deeper, IA focuses on structuring content in a manner that users can understand. Think of it as creating a roadmap for a website, app, or system. This structure, often represented as site maps, hierarchies, or flows, ensures that as users navigate a digital platform, their experience is intuitive and logical.

Practical Examples

Wikipedia's Category System: notice the neat categories at the bottom of a Wikipedia page, that's IA in action, organizing vast amounts of information into digestible chunks for easy navigation.

E-Commerce Website Filters: On shopping sites, the filters that let you sort products by type, brand, size, or color? That's stellar IA, ensuring you find that perfect pair of shoes without sifting through thousands of unrelated items.

News Websites: With sections like World, Politics, Business, and more, news websites organize a deluge of daily content into intuitive sections, letting readers zero in on topics of interest.

Potential Pitfalls

The journey through Information Architecture isn't always smooth sailing. A complex structure can emerge as a significant pitfall if the IA is too convoluted or doesn't align with user expectations and mental models. Missteps in structuring information or neglecting to consider the various ways different user demographics navigate digital spaces can inadvertently create a cumbersome user experience. Additionally, maintaining a static IA without accommodating the evolving content or user needs can lead to an outdated and ineffective digital space.

Emerging Trends and Future Outlook

With the explosion of digital content, the need for effective IA is more crucial than ever. Newer trends like voice-activated systems and virtual reality platforms pose unique challenges, necessitating innovative IA solutions. Ethically, as AI gets integrated into IA tools, there's a growing concern about transparency and bias in automated categorization. Nevertheless, the future holds a more personalized, AI-driven, and seamless navigational experience, tailored to individual user behaviors and preferences.

Chapter 23 - Product Manager (PM)
The driver steering the wheel

Have you ever wondered who decides the features of your favorite app or how it should behave? Meet the Product Manager (PM) – the maestro who orchestrates a product's journey from idea to launch. They are the visionaries who imagine what a product could be and then guide teams to make that vision a reality.

Product Managers are the pivotal figures who orchestrate the product life cycle, from the initial concept, through development, to the final product, ensuring every element aligns with the user's needs and business goals. A PM collaborates with numerous departments, from design to engineering to marketing, ensuring everyone's working towards a common goal. Their role encompasses understanding user needs, defining product strategies, setting priorities, and monitoring progress. They're often seen as the bridge between technical teams and the business, ensuring the product aligns with both user needs and business goals.

Practical Examples

Releasing a New App Feature: Imagine Instagram launching "Reels." PMs would oversee the entire process, ensuring the feature's design, functionality, and usability align with user expectations and business objectives, all while coordinating with designers, developers, and marketers.

Revamping a Website: Consider Airbnb's website overhaul. A PM would have managed the redesign, ensuring user experience is enhanced, technical requirements are met, and the new design aligns with the overall business strategy.

Launching a Wearable Device: Envisage the release of the Apple Watch. A PM would lead the project, ensuring the hardware, software, design, and functionalities coalesce seamlessly, providing a stellar user experience while adhering to Apple's business goals.

Potential Pitfalls

The Product Manager's road might be strewn with hurdles, like unclear communication amongst interdisciplinary teams, misalignment between user needs and product features, or an imbalance between technical feasibility and design aspirations. PMs might grapple with prioritizing features, adhering to timelines, and managing resources efficiently, whilst ensuring the final product doesn't deviate from its intended utility and user experience.

Emerging Trends and Future Outlook

The digital landscape is ever-evolving, and PMs are at the forefront of navigating these changes. With advancements in AI and machine learning, PMs are now harnessing these tools to better predict user needs and automate tasks. Ethical considerations, especially concerning user data and privacy, are becoming paramount. In the future, we might see PMs specializing further, focusing on areas like sustainability or ethical tech, ensuring products not only meet user needs but also contribute positively to the world.

Chapter 24 - Product Designer
Crafting Digital Experiences

Ever marveled at how intuitive and beautiful your favorite app feels? Behind every swipe, tap, and transition lies the meticulous craft of a Product Designer. These are the artists and architects of the digital realm, crafting interfaces that are not just visually pleasing but also functionally seamless.

A Product Designer's role goes beyond mere aesthetics. As we've seen in the UX and UI chapter, designers intertwine user needs with business goals, using tools like wireframes, prototypes, and user flows. Their designs ensure that digital experiences are intuitive, accessible, and delightful, ultimately leading users on a journey where each interaction feels natural and purposeful.

Practical Examples

Spotify's Wrapped Feature: The Product Designers collaborate to create a visually captivating, personalized journey through users' listening habits, ensuring every slide is not just informative but also shareable and engaging.

Google Maps: The design guides users through physical space digitally, ensuring that information is presented clearly, actions like route selection are intuitive, and additional features (like restaurant reviews) are integrated seamlessly.

Duolingo: Designers harmonize playful visuals with a structured learning pathway, ensuring that users are engaged while the UI guides them effectively through their language learning journey.

Potential Pitfalls

Embarking on the journey of Product Design, one might navigate through some common challenges, like misinterpreting user needs, creating visually appealing designs that may not be functionally coherent, or neglecting accessibility. Balancing aesthetic allure with practical utility and inclusivity can be a delicate dance, where the misalignment of one can cascade into a subpar user experience.

Emerging Trends and Future Outlook

The future for Product Designers is both challenging and exciting. With the rise of Augmented and Virtual Reality, designers are exploring 3D and spatial design. Accessibility is becoming non-negotiable, ensuring every user, regardless of their physical or cognitive abilities, can access digital products. There's also a strong ethical dimension emerging: designers are increasingly tasked with creating products that not only serve users but also respect their time, attention, and well-being.

Chapter 25 - Quality Assurance (QA)

To the Conquer of Flawless Software

Ever used an app or software and thought, "Wow, this works perfectly!"? You likely have a QA team to thank for that seamless experience. They're the gatekeepers, ensuring that what's delivered to you is free from glitches and performs as intended.

Diving deeper, QA isn't just about finding bugs. It's a systematic process that assesses software quality and ensures it meets specified requirements before release. This involves creating detailed test plans, executing them, and documenting results. The ultimate goal? To provide confidence that the product being released is of the highest possible quality.

Practical Examples

Microsoft Windows Updates: Think about the extensive testing required before rolling out updates to millions of computers globally. QA teams ensure that these updates won't crash systems or cause software conflicts.

Mobile Banking Apps: With sensitive data at play, QA plays a pivotal role in ensuring transactions are smooth, data remains secure, and the user experience remains top-notch.

SpaceX Launch Software: In environments where errors can lead to multimillion-dollar losses, QA ensures that the software guiding rockets and spacecraft is foolproof.

Potential Pitfalls

Assuming uniform user navigation and failing to test diverse user paths can lead to undiscovered bugs, resulting in poor user experiences and, eventually, a decline in user engagement and trust.

Sometimes, teams may just focus on the most apparent functions during testing, neglecting edge cases, which can turn minor unnoticed bugs into glaring issues post-launch.
While ensuring a software works is pivotal, neglecting non-functional testing such as performance, usability, and reliability testing can lead to suboptimal user experiences, even if the software works flawlessly at a functional level.

Emerging Trends and Future Outlook

Automation is changing the face of QA. With tools like Selenium or Appium, repetitive tasks are automated, allowing QAs to focus on more complex challenges.

Additionally, the integration of AI is helping predict where issues might arise, even before they do. Ethical considerations are also paramount, ensuring software respects user data and privacy. As we move forward, QA remains a crucial layer, ensuring the software backbone of our digital age remains robust and trustworthy.

Chapter 26 - Agile
Is It Just a Buzzword or a Game-Changer in Software Development?

"Agile" isn't just a buzzword that's been making the rounds in tech circles; it's a philosophy, a way of approaching project management and product development that's about being efficient, adaptive, and user-focused. Imagine building a car while driving it; you start with the basics - wheels and a frame, enough to get moving. As you roll forward, you continually enhance it, adding an engine, seats, and maybe a snazzy paint job while adapting to the evolving needs and challenges that appear on your journey. That, in a nutshell, is Agile: starting with a "Minimum Viable Product" (MVP) and iteratively building upon it based on continuous feedback and evolving requirements.

Agile represents a set of principles and values for software development under which requirements and solutions evolve through the collaborative effort of self-organizing cross-functional teams. It advocates adaptive planning, evolutionary development, early delivery, and continual improvement, and it encourages rapid and flexible response to change.

Practical Examples

Spotify: The music streaming giant uses Agile methodologies to constantly enhance user experience, releasing frequent updates that refine features and introduce new ones, ensuring they're always in tune with user needs and market dynamics.

ING: The Dutch banking group restructured its entire organization to work in an Agile manner, organizing teams into squads and tribes to enhance flexibility and customer focus, enabling them to adapt quickly to the fast-changing financial industry.

3. Potential Pitfalls

Agile can sometimes be misinterpreted or improperly implemented. One potential pitfall is forsaking proper planning under the guise of "being Agile." This methodology isn't about bypassing structured planning but rather about maintaining flexibility within planned parameters. Another common misconception is thinking that Agile means no documentation. In reality, Agile emphasizes value-creating activities and considers excessive documentation as non-value-adding, but it still necessitates adequate documentation. Furthermore, effective implementation of Agile demands a cultural shift in organizations which can be challenging to navigate, involving adjustments in roles, workflows, and communication.

4. Emerging Trends and Future Outlook

The realm of Agile is extending beyond software development and embedding itself into organizational structures and workflows across various industries. We're witnessing the emergence of "Business Agility" - applying Agile principles universally across an organization, not just in product development. With the ever-escalating pace of technological and market changes, Agile's adaptability and customer-centricity become even more crucial, hinting towards a future where its principles become integral across diverse sectors and functions.

Chapter 27 - Scrum

The current standard for "cooking" Software

Imagine you're trying to bake the perfect cake, but you've never done it before. Instead of throwing in all the ingredients and hoping for the best, wouldn't it be wiser to add a bit, taste, and adjust as you go? That's the essence of Scrum: it's a framework within which people can address complex adaptive problems, while productively and creatively delivering products of the highest possible value. It's like cooking with the freedom to modify the recipe - incrementally and iteratively improving as you continue cooking.

Scrum is a framework that provides structure, discipline, and a pathway for improvement. Essentially, Scrum breaks down the production process into small, manageable pieces (called "sprints") with regular check-ins (daily standups) and reviews to ensure that the work is on the right track.

Real-world Examples

3M: This global conglomerate applied Scrum to improve efficiency in their Post-it note development processes, resulting in faster time-to-market and innovative product features.

BBC: The British broadcasting company employed Scrum in redesigning their website, ensuring user needs were continuously met and adapting to feedback swiftly.

Adobe: When creating its Creative Cloud services, Adobe embraced Scrum. The result was rapid feature releases and the ability to quickly respond to market demands.

Potential Pitfalls

Embarking on the Scrum journey isn't without its challenges. Misunderstanding the framework often leads to misapplication. For instance, Scrum doesn't mean disregarding management or oversight; instead, it redefines leadership roles. Another pitfall is considering Scrum as a solution to all problems. Scrum is powerful, but it isn't a one-size-fits-all answer and needs to be adapted considering organizational needs. Lastly, while Scrum advocates flexibility, it does require adherence to its key principles and roles, often demanding a cultural shift that might be resisted within organizations.

Emerging Trends and Future Outlook

Scrum's efficacy isn't limited to software. Industries from education to marketing are adopting its principles for project management and product development. As remote work becomes more prevalent, virtual Scrum tools and techniques are gaining traction. Ethically, Scrum's emphasis on regular reflection promotes a culture of continuous improvement, pushing teams towards excellence. The future promises a broader adoption of Scrum as organizations realize the benefits of iterative development and team collaboration.

Chapter 28 - API

The Secret Correspondence Behind Apps and Websites

Have you ever wondered how apps like weather services fetch updates or how your favorite travel booking sites compare prices from various airlines? Think of APIs as secret messengers—running back and forth between applications, carrying your requests for information and then returning with the desired data. At the surface, you see a smooth experience; behind the scenes, it's the API working its magic.

Diving deeper, an API specifies the methods and data formats applications should use to communicate. It's like a menu in a restaurant: you make a choice (request), the kitchen (server) prepares the dish, and then it's brought to you (response). APIs can be public (open to external developers) or private (restricted to internal use), making them versatile tools in the realm of software.

Practical Examples

Google Maps API: Ever noticed maps embedded in a store locator page on a company's website? That's the Google Maps API at work, allowing businesses to integrate Google's map services into their own applications.

Twitter API: Social media platforms like Twitter allow third-party apps to fetch user data, post tweets, or gather trending topics, all through their API.

Payment APIs (Stripe): Online shopping made easy. These APIs handle secure money transactions, allowing online stores to process payments without storing card details.

Potential Pitfalls

Navigating through APIs may pose some challenges. One of which is managing API changes. If a third-party API changes its rules or endpoints, it may break the functionalities of your application. API rate limiting can be another hurdle; some APIs restrict the number of requests you can make in a set period. Security is also paramount; insecure API can expose sensitive data to malicious entities, necessitating robust security practices to safeguard information.

Emerging Trends and Future Outlook

In the future tapestry of tech, APIs are weaving more intricate and versatile patterns. The emergence of API-first design, where APIs are designed before the software that uses them, underscores their centrality in software development. APIs are becoming increasingly vital in enabling Machine Learning capabilities, providing essential data and functionalities without an extensive foundational build. Moreover, the surge in Microservices Architecture – developing applications as a collection of loosely coupled, independently deployable services – is elevating the importance of APIs in ensuring these microservices communicate and function harmoniously. APIs are crucial cogs in the digital ecosystem, and their relevance and application are poised to permeate deeper into various technological domains.

Chapter 29 - Migration

Ever Moved House? Imagine Software Doing That!

Has the stress of shifting to a new house, packing all belongings and ensuring they reach the destination safely, ever overwhelmed you? In the digital world, software and systems often have to undergo a similar "relocation" - this is called migration. At a high level, migration is about moving data, applications, or entire IT processes from one environment to another, typically to access better technology or to streamline operations.

Technically, migration might involve transferring from an on-premises data center to a cloud platform, moving from one database system to another, or even upgrading to a newer software version. It's a complex process, often requiring thorough planning and strategies to minimize disruptions and data losses. As technology evolves, migration ensures systems remain current, efficient, and secure.

Practical Examples

Database Migrations: A company might transfer its data from an older database system, say MySQL, to a newer or more suitable one like PostgreSQL, to enhance performance or utilize specific features.

Website Platform Shifts: Websites may move from one content management system to another (like Joomla to WordPress) to offer a better user experience or easier content management.

Potential Pitfalls

Migration is not without its challenges. Data loss is a prominent risk during migrations, ensuring every bit is transferred and none is left behind is crucial. Downtime is another significant concern; businesses often can't afford to halt operations during migration, requiring meticulous planning to ensure continuity. Moreover, unexpected costs and complexity in managing the new environment, especially if staff aren't trained to navigate it, can pose notable hurdles in migration endeavors.

Emerging Trends and Future Outlook

As cloud adoption accelerates, cloud migration services are in high demand, with tools emerging to automate and streamline the process. Containerization, using technologies like Docker, is simplifying application migrations, ensuring consistency across different environments. With the rise of hybrid-cloud and multi-cloud strategies, inter-cloud migrations are becoming more prevalent. Ethically, migrations must prioritize data integrity and security, ensuring users' information isn't compromised during transitions. As we progress, expect migration tasks to be more frequent, yet smoother, with refined tools and best practices guiding the way.

Module 3 Closing

Module 3 has granted us an intricate view into the world of Software Development, blending technical acumen with human-centric designs and strategic practices.

Let's recap on the field that crafts our digital world.

Creating Digital Experiences: Front-end Development crafts visual digital experiences and ensures user interactions are intuitive, engaging, and inclusive.

Powering User Interactions: Back-End Development is more than managing server-side operations; it's the engine that powers, secures, and ensures reliability in the digital experiences we interact with.

Designing with Empathy: UX and UI Design weave together not only the aesthetic and functional aspects of digital products but also ensure they are empathetically aligned with user needs and behaviors.

Understanding Users Deeply: User Research is diving deep into understanding user behaviors, needs, and motivations to shape human-centric designs and strategies.

Organizing Digital Information: Information Architecture extends beyond organizing content and information but also ensures a coherent, intuitive, and user-friendly navigation through digital spaces.

Guiding Product Success: The Product Manager navigates not just through product development processes but also ensures that products are strategically positioned for success in competitive markets.

Crafting Product Visions: The Product Designer doesn't just design products but crafts visions into tangible, user-friendly, and aesthetic digital solutions.

Ensuring Digital Excellence: QA (Quality Assurance) is more than finding bugs. It ensures a product's excellence, reliability, and optimal performance in the hands of users.

Adaptable Development: Agile isn't merely a development methodology but a philosophy that embraces adaptability, continuous improvement, and user-centeredness in product development.

Focused Project Delivery: Scrum goes beyond being a framework and serves as a catalyst for focused, incremental, and collaborative project delivery.

Connecting Software Components: API is not only about connecting software components but enabling systems to communicate, share data, and function harmoniously.

Strategizing Data Movement: Migration involves strategizing, securing, and ensuring the integrity of data as it transitions between systems or formats.

Ready for the next big thing?

Module 4 - Artificial Intelligence. The Next (now!) big thing.

Remember when the phrase 'Artificial Intelligence' only conjured up images of sinister robots in sci-fi movies or perhaps that car in the Knight Rider TV show? Well, AI has evolved, and it's not just about those robots with its own personality but on a complete revolution of our office and creative tools as well as the entertainment subscriptions we watch and listen to. In fact, it's become a part of our daily life in ways we might not even realize. Ever wondered how streaming services recommend shows or how virtual assistants understand what song you're in the mood for? That's AI!

In this module, we're going on an exciting ride through the next big thing that is going mainstream in 2022 with the rise of generative AI and other products made with Artificial Intelligence. We'll demystify terms like Machine Learning and Deep Learning, and even introduce you to some familiar AI personalities—like Chatbots.

So, whether you've just stepped out of your time machine from the 1990s or you're the tech-savvy millennial who thinks they've got it all down, strap in! This AI journey is bound to surprise you.

Chapter 30: Machine Learning.

When Computers Get Schooled.

Have you ever marveled at how your email knows what's junk and what's not without you even whispering a word? That's Machine Learning (ML) waltzing through your email. ML is like teaching computers to learn from experience. Imagine teaching your dog a new trick: you'd reward him with treats whenever he gets it right until eventually, he just gets it. Similarly, ML involves feeding the computer data (the experiences) and allowing it to learn patterns and make decisions from it.

Machine Learning is a subset of artificial intelligence that provides systems the ability to automatically learn and improve from experience without being explicitly programmed. This learning process is based on the recognition of complex patterns in data and the making of intelligent decisions based on them.

Practical Examples

Email Filtering: Your email filters spam not because it knows what spam looks like, but because it's learned from millions of examples what spammy emails tend to look like.

Voice Assistants: When Siri or Alexa accurately catches your command to play your favorite song, that's ML in action, recognizing patterns in your speech from heaps of voice data.

Recommendation Systems: Ever wondered how Netflix suggests movies that are just your type? ML algorithms use your watching history and similar users' history to make smart, tailored suggestions.

Potential Pitfalls

Despite its wonders, ML isn't devoid of challenges. For one, it needs vast amounts of data to learn effectively, and sometimes, obtaining this data is a mountainous task. Plus, there's the risk of bias – if the learning data contains biases, the ML model will likely perpetuate them. Furthermore, ML models can sometimes be like black boxes, making decisions without humans fully understanding how they were derived.

Emerging Trends and Future Outlook

The future of ML glimmers with possibilities. We're looking at even more personalized experiences, like mood-based music playlists or health apps predicting a cold before you even sneeze. But, on the flip side, as ML permeates our lives, ethical use of our data, preventing bias in ML models, and ensuring transparency and explainability in decisions made by machines will take center stage in discussions and policies. The journey ahead is spectacular yet warrants a mindful approach to navigate through the entwining vines of innovation and ethics.

Chapter 31: Generative AI
When Computers Get Creative!

Ever watched a movie and thought, "I could write a better dialogue than that!" Well, Generative AI might just beat you to the punchline, and possibly craft a whimsical one at that! Generative AI is like that talented artist in the digital world, which doesn't just recognize or analyze content but creates new, never-seen-before stuff. It's that creative mind, but in algorithms and computations.

Zooming in technically, Generative AI refers to models that use neural networks to produce new content, whether it be text, images, or music, that's similar to, but not exactly like, the content it was trained on. It isn't merely processing or analyzing data; it's making something entirely new from its learning.

Practical Examples

ChatGPT: Perhaps you've heard of ChatGPT, creating impressively coherent and contextually relevant responses in a conversation, without having specific pre-written answers.

DeepArt: DeepArt takes style from one image and applies it to others, turning your selfie into a Picasso-esque masterpiece without a literal stroke of effort!

JukeBox by OpenAI: An AI model that can generate music, complete with lyrics and vocals, in various styles and genres, hitting those notes in a truly tech-savvy style.

3. Potential Pitfalls

Generative AI is undeniably mesmerizing but comes with its fair share of concerns. The risk of generating deceptive or manipulative content, like deep fakes, is real and can pose ethical and social challenges. Plus, ensuring the AI creates something that adheres to ethical and societal norms (imagine avoiding bias in text or appropriateness in images) is a tough nut to crack. Not to mention, the legal conundrums related to copyrights when AI starts creating art, music, or literature.

Emerging Trends and Future Outlook

From writing novels to designing fashion collections, Generative AI is stretching its creative muscles everywhere. But as with all arts, there's a debate about authenticity. Can machine-made art capture human emotions? Will the next bestselling novel be written by a computer? Only time will tell!

And while it's all very sci-fi and exciting, we must tread carefully. Ensuring that AI-created content is ethical and doesn't infringe on copyrights or spread misinformation is crucial.

So, next time you see a jaw-dropping artwork or hear a catchy tune, ask yourself: was a human or a computer the genius behind it? Intriguing, right?

Chapter 32: Prompts

Whispering to AIs, and They Respond!

Prompts are like conversation starters for artificial intelligence. In essence, they're instructions or questions that we feed to an AI, guiding it to produce specific outputs. Think of it as tossing a question into the vast digital ocean of an AI's brain and watching as it fishes out an answer tailored just for you. Yes, you're having a chat with a machine!

Technically, when you use a prompt, the AI accesses its vast training data, processes the instruction, and offers a response that aligns with the nudge you gave it. In the realm of language models like GPT, prompts help in specifying a task without altering the model itself. It's like asking politely and directly to get what you want!.

Practical Examples

Copywriting Assistants: AI copywriting tools use prompts like "Create a catchy slogan for a vegan chocolate brand" to generate creative, niche-specific content.

Coding Helper: For coding assistance, a prompt might look like, "Write a Python function to calculate factorial of a number," and voila, the AI provides you with a handy snippet!

Language Translation: In translation tools, "Translate the following English text to French: [Text]" acts as a prompt to guide the AI in performing the desired translation.

Potential Pitfalls

Prompts seem straightforward but crafting a good one can be an art and a science. Too vague, and the AI might stroll aimlessly in the wrong direction. Too specific, and you might stifle its creative capabilities. Plus, there's the risk of biased or undesired outputs if the prompts unknowingly contain inherent biases or misleading cues.

Emerging Trends and Future Outlook

Peering into the future, prompts will likely become even more crucial as our digital assistants get more advanced and multifaceted. Imagine having a digital "friend" where your casual, colloquial chats become prompts that guide it to perform various tasks – from crafting poems to solving mathematical conundrums. The effectiveness of our interaction with advanced AI will hinge significantly on how well we master the art of prompting. It's like having a genie in a bottle, where your wishes (prompts) need to be just right to get what you desire!

Chapter 33: Chatbots

Who's behind "Hello, How Can I Help?"

How many of us have been caught conversing with those friendly online chat pop-ups thinking, "Is this a human or a robot?" It's like being in a sci-fi movie where you're unsure if the person you're talking to is real. Welcome to the chatbot revolution! Chatbots are those tireless digital assistants who always seem eager to help, 24/7, rain or shine.

In essence, chatbots are software applications designed to simulate human conversation. Whether it's through text or voice, they communicate with users, assist them in completing tasks, answer inquiries, or just engage in casual banter. They often live in messaging apps and are engineered to understand and respond based on both pre-set rules and AI-powered learning.

Practical Examples

Customer Service: Businesses use chatbots to answer frequently asked questions, guide users through processes, and provide immediate responses at any hour of the day.

Virtual Assistants: Think Siri or Alexa - these chatbots not only answer queries but control other tech aspects, like playing your favorite tune or checking the weather.

Healthcare Bots: In healthcare, chatbots might assist in scheduling appointments, sending medication reminders, or even providing basic health advice.

Potential Pitfalls

Although helpful, chatbots do not always have the answers. Misunderstandings can occur, and chatbots may fail to comprehend complex instructions or nuances of human conversation. And well, dealing with an annoyed user? That's an art bots are still mastering. Then, there's the privacy conundrum – ensuring these virtual chatters protect and respect user data is paramount.

Emerging Trends and Future Outlook

Chatting with bots is only going to get more sophisticated. Future chatbots will likely understand us way better, deciphering the moods and nuances from our messages, and responding with empathy or appropriate humor.

Imagine chatbots that not only assist but also sense when you've had a rough day, offering a virtual ear or a chuckle-worthy joke.

Chatbots are already changing massively how we work and create. Did you know this book has been co-written and proofread with a Chatbot? Have you heard of ChatGPT yet?

ChatGPT is probably the most advanced chatbot out there and a revolution in generative AI. Check-it out yourself at chatgpt.openai.com and play with any of the prompts and ways to use the chatbot that you will be presented with.

Get ready to experience generative AI.

Chapter 34: Natural Language Processing (NLP)

Teaching machines to understand us

You're in a foreign country and you don't speak the local language. Amidst the cacophony of unfamiliar words, you're trying to buy the juiciest mangoes. A kind local, observes your gestures, tone, and expressions, successfully hands you the finest pick! Now, Natural Language Processing (NLP) is somewhat like that kind of local, but in the digital domain, making sense of the cacophony of our human language and ensuring smooth communication with machines.

NLP is a branch of AI that focuses on the interaction between computers and humans through natural language. Its ultimate objective is to read, decipher, and make sense of human language in a manner that is valuable. It blends linguistic understanding with artificial intelligence to enable machines to comprehend text, hear speech, interpret it, measure sentiment, and determine which parts are important.

Practical Examples

Search Engines: When you type a query into Google, NLP helps decipher what you're looking for and provides relevant results.

Translation Services: Apps like Google Translate utilize NLP to convert text or speech from one language to another, bridging communication gaps across languages.

Speech Recognition: Voice-activated assistants, like Siri or Alexa, use NLP to understand and act upon your verbal commands.

Potential Pitfalls

Navigating the nuanced lanes of human language is no piece of cake for NLP. Sarcasm, cultural contexts, regional dialects, and varying tones can trip it up, leading to misinterpretations and misguided responses. Another stumbling block is the continuous evolution of language, with new slang, phrases, and expressions popping up continually, making it a never-ending learning curve for our digital interpreters.

Emerging Trends and Future Outlook

Venturing forward, NLP is set to break down even more language barriers, enriching our interactions with machines and facilitating more authentic, understanding conversations. It will likely delve deeper into deciphering emotional undertones, context-appropriate responses, and maybe, just maybe, understanding that aubergine emojis can imply more than just discussing vegetables.

Future iterations of NLP will continue to enhance our technological interactions, bridging gaps not just in language, but also in understanding and connection, ushering us into an era where your tech not only comprehends your words but also, to some extent, "gets" you.

Chapter 35: Computer Vision

Eyes of the Algorithm that Perceive and Interpret

Imagine you're an enthusiastic tourist, exploring a historic town with your camera. You capture vibrant photos, appreciating the architecture, people, and colors through your lens. Computer Vision (CV) mimics this experience, but it goes one step further: it not only "sees" the visuals but also comprehends them.

Computer Vision is a subfield of artificial intelligence that trains computers to interpret and make decisions based on visual data, just like humans do. It empowers computers to extract, analyze, and understand useful information from images or video. From recognizing objects and classifying them, to detecting anomalies or even predicting actions, CV works to make sense of visual input in a meaningful way.

Practical Examples

Face Recognition: Social media platforms using CV to identify and tag people in photos.

Healthcare Imaging: Using CV to detect abnormalities in X-rays or MRI images to aid diagnosis.

Autonomous Vehicles: Cars utilizing CV to navigate roads safely by identifying obstacles, traffic signals, and pedestrians.

Potential Pitfalls

Compture Vision can sometimes struggle with contextual nuances and minute details that the human eye can naturally distinguish. Differentiating between objects with similar appearances or understanding scenes with complex backgrounds and multiple elements can be challenging. Additionally, ethical concerns, such as privacy infringements through unwarranted use of facial recognition technologies, also pose significant challenges and call for robust guidelines and regulations.

Emerging Trends and Future Outlook

Stepping into the future, the lens of computer vision is set to broaden and refine. From advanced facial recognition that respects ethical and privacy norms to comprehensive healthcare solutions that predict issues before they visibly manifest — the future of CV is illuminating. We might see CV collaborating with other tech domains, providing visually intuitive solutions that enrich our digital interactions, ensuring that technology not only "sees" our world but also understands and respects its complexities and nuances. So, in essence, our digital realm will not just witness but also wisely interpret the vibrant, chaotic, and beautiful tapestry of our visual world.

Chapter 36: Neuronal Network
Digital brains

Imagine teaching a group of toddlers to identify various shapes. You might show them numerous instances of each shape until they can discern a circle from a square or a triangle from a rectangle. Similarly, in the digital realm, Neural Networks work on a comparable principle but within a complex, intricate web of learning nodes.

A Neural Network is a series of algorithms that recognizes underlying relationships in a set of data through a process that mimics the way the human brain operates. These networks consist of layers of nodes, akin to neurons, and they learn from data by altering the weights of inputs, continuously adjusting until the output is as accurate as possible. It's like honing the instincts of our digital toddlers, refining their understanding through repeated practice and subtle adjustments.

Practical Examples

Stock Market Predictions: Analyzing trends and patterns to predict future stock values and make strategic investment decisions.

Image Recognition: Training systems to identify and categorize images, such as differentiating between cat and dog photos.

Voice Assistants: Adapting and improving responses by understanding varied accents and speech nuances across users.

Potential Pitfalls

Neural Networks, while impressively robust, are not without their challenges. The accuracy and reliability of their predictions are profoundly dependent on the quality and quantity of data fed into them. Any inconsistency or bias in the data can adversely affect their outcomes. Moreover, they require substantial computing power and can sometimes act as a "black box," offering predictions without transparent reasoning or clear interpretability.

Emerging Trends and Future Outlook

Envisaging the future, Neural Networks will likely weave into numerous sectors, offering predictive insights and nuanced understandings with even more precision. From healthcare, providing diagnostic predictions and treatment suggestions, to the entertainment industry, customizing user experiences with keen accuracy, the applications are boundless. The ongoing refinement of Neural Networks promises a future where our digital entities can predict, adapt, and respond with striking intuition and acute accuracy, bridging the gap between technological function and human-like understanding even further.

Chapter 37: Deep Fake
When Reality Gets a Makeover

It's unnerving to see a video of a world leader singing pop songs or confessing to alien encounters, especially when you find out the video isn't real but looks astoundingly so. Welcome to the world of Deepfakes! A fusion of "deep learning" and "fake", Deepfakes use sophisticated AI and Neural Networks to create hyper-realistic but entirely fake content, where individuals appear to say or do things they've never done.

Deepfakes harness machine learning to superimpose existing images or videos onto source media. The technology essentially teaches a computer to superimpose one face onto another, learning and applying intricate facial features and expressions. From swapping faces of celebrities to generating speaking avatars of historical figures, it's a tech marvel, albeit one with potential for misuse.

Practical Examples

Entertainment Industry: Bringing deceased actors back to the screen by superimposing their faces on live actors.

Social Media Fun: Creating fun and engaging videos where users swap faces with celebrities or animate static photos.

Historical Recreations: Producing speeches or appearances of historical figures in museums or documentaries.

Potential Pitfalls

Despite the awe-inspiring capabilities, Deepfakes pose a lot of ethical issues and are going to be a nightmare over coming years to discern real information from misinformation. The ease with which individuals can be made to appear to say or do things they haven't, propels deepfakes to the forefront of a lot of fake news and manipulation. The technology can be misused for creating misleading videos, spreading disinformation, or malicious impersonation, all of which can have substantial real-world consequences. Verifying the authenticity of such content and establishing regulatory frameworks stand as burgeoning challenges.

Emerging Trends and Future Outlook

In a future where seeing is not necessarily believing, technologies to detect and counteract Deepfakes are on a steep rise. Deepfakes could evolve to become even more convincing and widely accessible, making the differentiation between real and synthetic media increasingly challenging.

On a positive note, Deepfake technology could also be used for benign and entertaining purposes, like revitalizing old movies, creating new content, or enhancing virtual reality experiences. The onus, it appears, is on striking a balance, ensuring ethical usage while safeguarding against potential misuses.

Module 4 Closing

Alright, let's take a brief pause and look back. We just navigated the vast ocean of Artificial Intelligence, here are the main takeaways:

Pioneering Possibilities: The domains of Machine Learning and AI bring forward not just algorithms and models but pioneering possibilities across industries.

Human and Machine Interplay: Through Generative AI and Chatbots, the interplay between human creativity and machine capability becomes more seamless and empowering.

Learning and Adapting: With frameworks like Neuronal Networks and technologies like Deep Learning, machines exhibit a remarkable ability to learn, adapt, and predict.

Ethical and Moral Compass: The advent of Deepfake technology highlights a poignant need for an ethical and moral compass in navigating the application of AI technologies.

Unveiling Nuances: Deep Learning and Machine Learning enable the extraction and understanding of patterns and nuances in vast datasets, unveiling insights and predictive capabilities.

Conversational Capacities: From Chatbots to ChatGPT, AI has breached the barriers of mere functionality to embrace conversational and contextual interactivity with users.

And remember, **AI** It's not just for tech nerds. AI is everywhere, from our phones to our fridges. It's changing industries, creating new ones, and redefining what's possible.

While AI can replicate many things, the human touch, our emotions, experiences, and nuances, remains irreplaceable. Let's appreciate AI for what it can do, but also cherish the things it can't replicate.

Just like the AI models that constantly learn and improve, we too should adopt a mindset of continuous learning, especially in this rapidly changing digital age.

You are half way through the book! Let's keep going?!

Module 5 - Data Analysis and Data Science. What are these data driven decisions?

You might be wondering, "Data...? Isn't that just... numbers?" Data is the secret sauce that powers most of the decisions in businesses today. From choosing the next movie you should watch to forecasting stock market trends, data is the magical wand waving behind the scenes.

In this module, we're about to discover the intricate maze of data analytics and data science. Think of it like your favorite detective series, but instead of hunting down culprits, we're deciphering insights and patterns. From SQL queries to get basic data to dynamic dashboards in Tableau that are more mesmerizing than modern art, this module will unveil the intelligence that's powering the 21st century.

Whether you're here to upskill for your job or just out of sheer curiosity, hang tight. There's a data story waiting for you.

Chapter 38: Data Analytics
Isn't it all just...numbers?

You might think back to your school days, squinting at numbers and wondering, "When am I ever going to use this?" The universe probably chuckled because, surprise, data has become the beating heart of modern businesses. But what's this all about? Well, data analytics is the art (and science) of examining raw data with the purpose of drawing conclusions about that information.

Take those numbers as puzzle pieces. Alone, they might not make much sense. But when you start connecting them, a clearer picture emerges. Data analytics involves a blend of various techniques, algorithms, and software to help these puzzles come to life. It's like being a detective, where numbers are your only witnesses. Your task? To interrogate them and extract insights.

Practical Examples

Marketing Campaigns: Ever wonder how companies know just the right moment to shoot you an email about a discount? That's data analytics at work. They've crunched the numbers from your browsing habits, past purchases, and even the time you're most likely to check your mail.

Healthcare: From predicting patient admissions to understanding the potential outbreaks of diseases, data analytics aids in better healthcare management and proactive treatments.

Finance: Predicting stock market trends, credit scores, and fraud detection, all lean heavily on data analytics. So if you've ever gotten an alert about a suspicious transaction, give a nod to the data wizards behind the scenes.

Potential Pitfalls

Now, while data analytics sounds like the crystal ball everyone needs, it's not without its challenges. The quality of insights is only as good as the data you feed into it. Inaccurate or biased data can lead to misleading results. Moreover, analyzing vast amounts of data requires powerful systems, and not every organization has access to these. Remember, while numbers don't lie, they can sometimes mislead if not interpreted with care and context.

Reflections and Takeaways

Data analytics, at its heart, is storytelling with numbers. It's an ongoing conversation between businesses and their environments, guiding them towards smarter, data-informed decisions. In a rapidly evolving world, those not tuning into this conversation might just be left behind. So, the next time you come across a statistic or chart, know there's a story behind it, and you've got the basic tools to understand it.

Chapter 39: MySQL
And what's with the SQL?

Do you ever find yourself wishing for an ultra-organized friend who remembers every tiny detail? Well, databases aim to be that ultra-efficient friend for information. They store, recall, and manage data, making life more organized for businesses.

MySQL stands tall among these databases, acting as a virtual super-organizer. MySQL is a relational database management system. At its essence, it's where applications store data so they can query and retrieve it efficiently. If databases were libraries, MySQL would be the organized librarian who knows exactly where each book belongs.

Practical Examples

Websites and Web Applications: Most of the websites you visit daily, from e-commerce platforms to blogs, use MySQL to manage their data.

Data Warehousing: Companies often collect massive amounts of data. MySQL helps in storing and retrieving this data swiftly. It acts like that warehouse manager.

E-commerce: Websites like Amazon or eBay have millions of products listed, with new ones added every minute. The details of these products, user reviews, and transaction histories are efficiently managed using MySQL.

Potential Pitfalls

But it's not all rainbows and unicorns with MySQL. It's essential to understand its limitations. As data scales up, sometimes MySQL can struggle to keep up with very high concurrent requests. Moreover, while it's amazing for structured data, the rise of unstructured data has seen other non-relational databases gain prominence.

Emerging Trends and Future Outlook

With cloud computing taking center stage, cloud-native versions of MySQL have become more prevalent. Companies are looking for managed solutions where they don't have to bother with the nitty-gritty of maintenance and can focus solely on their application. Additionally, the demand for real-time analytics is pushing MySQL to evolve and integrate better with big data solutions.

Chapter 40: Tableau and Looker
The Magical Duo of Data Visualization

What's all the fuss about? Tableau and Looker are top-tier data visualization tools that help businesses understand their data by turning it into interactive visuals. Imagine having a giant box of Lego pieces. Raw data is like that - lots of potential but a bit chaotic. Now, Tableau and Looker are your master Lego builders, who take those pieces and craft them into epic castles and spaceships, but for this case into great visualizations and charts.

These tools come packed with features that allow users to create dashboards, reports, and more without the need for programming. They can pull data from various sources, from Excel to cloud databases, and transform it into charts, graphs, and heat maps. It's all about making data accessible, understandable, and actionable.

Practical Applications

Sales Performance: Imagine being a sales manager. With a quick glance at a Tableau dashboard, you can identify which regions or clients are performing well.

Market Trends: For marketing folks, Looker can highlight the most effective campaigns, track user engagement, and predict future market trends. No more guesswork!

Operational Efficiency: Operations teams can easily spot inefficiencies, like which processes take too long or where costs are mounting.

Potential Pitfalls

Sure, Tableau and Looker are amazing, but no tool is without its quirks. For one, there's a learning curve. You can't just jump in and expect to craft a Mona Lisa on day one. Data preparation and cleaning can also be time-consuming. And, as with any tool, if the data going in isn't of high quality, the visuals coming out won't be much help.

Emerging Trends and Future Outlook

Data visualization tools are evolving at a rapid pace. With the rise of AI and machine learning, platforms like Tableau and Looker are becoming smarter, offering predictive analytics features and automated insights. Integration capabilities are expanding too, making it easier to connect to various data sources.

In the future, we might see even more immersive data experiences, perhaps blending with augmented or virtual reality. Imagine walking through a 3D graph or interacting with data in a holographic space. The future of data visualization is not just on our screens but all around us.

Chapter 41: Business Intelligence
Decoding the Business Crystal Ball

"Did you ever wish for a crystal ball during those indecisive moments in life? 'Should I buy this? Should I invest in that?' Well, in the business world, there's something that comes pretty close. It's called Business Intelligence (BI).

Business Intelligence is all about collecting, analyzing, and visualizing business data to aid decision-making. Think of it as a magnifying glass that zooms into every nook and cranny of a company, illuminating hidden trends, patterns, and insights.

BI tools take raw data - sales numbers, customer reviews, inventory levels, and so on - and churn out meaningful insights.The result? More informed decisions, strategic moves, and a clearer vision of the future.

Practical Examples

Inventory Management: Retail businesses can use BI to analyze sales patterns, forecast demand, and ensure they never overstock or run out of products.

Customer Insights: E-commerce sites can dig into customer behavior, understand preferences, and tailor experiences to boost sales.

Performance Benchmarks: Companies can compare their performance against industry standards or competitors, helping them spot areas of improvement.

Potential Pitfalls

As captivating as BI sounds, it's not all sunshine and rainbows. For starters, just because you have insights doesn't mean you'll always make the right decisions. Data interpretation is key! Additionally, a common mistake is over-relying on BI and ignoring intuition or human judgment. And remember, garbage in equals garbage out. If you feed BI systems with poor-quality data, expect skewed insights in return.

Emerging Trends and Future Outlook

BI is on a journey of evolution. Increasing integration of AI means BI tools are becoming more intuitive and predictive. The future might see BI not just showing us the data, but also suggesting specific actionable strategies.

There's also a trend towards 'self-service BI', where non-techies can easily access and interpret data without needing IT specialists. This democratization ensures that insights aren't just locked with a select few but are available across an organization.

With every chart, graph, and insight, companies are not just seeing their present clearer but also charting a path for a smarter future.

Chapter 42: Data Science and Data Engineering

The Dynamic Duo of the Data World

Imagine building a house. The data engineer is the person who lays down the foundation, sets up the electrical wiring, and ensures the plumbing's in place. They manage and optimize databases to handle and query data efficiently.

On the other hand, Data Science is like the interior designer of that house. They take the structure, and using their tools (like Machine Learning algorithms), they transform that raw data into meaningful insights. They're the ones making the data "livable," converting it into actionable advice for businesses.

Practical Examples

Streaming Services: Ever wonder how Netflix knows what you want to watch next? Data engineers ensure the platform can handle millions of users, while data scientists analyze viewing patterns to recommend the next binge-worthy show.

E-commerce: When you shop online, data engineers make sure your experience is smooth. Data scientists, meanwhile, analyze your browsing habits to suggest products you might like.

Healthcare: Data engineers manage vast amounts of patient data, ensuring easy access for doctors. Data scientists use this data to predict outbreaks or devise better treatment strategies.

Potential Pitfalls

These roles are invaluable, but not without challenges. For data engineers, ensuring data privacy and security is paramount. One small breach, and sensitive information can be exposed. For data scientists, there's the challenge of 'overfitting' – where their models work incredibly well on the data they have but fail miserably with new data. It's a delicate dance between making accurate models and ensuring they're adaptable.

Emerging Trends and Future Outlook

The data world is always evolving. Data engineering is moving towards real-time data processing, while data science is getting a boost from deep learning, making predictions even more accurate. Furthermore, with businesses realizing the synergy between the two, expect more integrated roles where data scientists possess engineering know-how and vice-versa.

Chapter 43: Big Data
The Era of Information Overload

Data, Data Everywhere: If you think of data as water, our digital age is nothing short of a torrential downpour. In this ceaseless rain, a few droplets won't make a difference, but the constant and overwhelming flow is what stands out. This vast, relentless influx is what we term as Big Data.

Big Data refers to extensive datasets, both structured like databases and unstructured like social media content, that are too large and complex to process through traditional methods we've seen like MySQL. What sets Big Data apart isn't just its size, but its variety, velocity, and volume. It's about the speed at which new data is generated and the diversity of information sources. Imagine a relentless stream of data coming from online purchases, social media interactions, electronic medical records, GPS signals, and even sensors tracking weather patterns. Such a diverse blend of information gives organizations an unprecedented opportunity to find new insights, optimize operations, and predict future trends. However, to truly leverage its power, we need advanced tools, techniques, and platforms to process, analyze, and interpret this data.

Practical Examples

Traffic Management: Modern GPS systems utilize Big Data to provide real-time traffic updates, analyzing data from countless vehicles and sensors to suggest the most efficient routes.

Retail and Loyalty Programs: Receive offers that seem uncannily precise? Retailers harness Big Data insights from purchase histories to refine and target their promotions more effectively.

Potential Pitfalls

Big Data isn't without its challenges. Storing, managing, and analyzing such vast data requires specialized solutions. Concerns about privacy are real and imminent; more data generally translates to increased risk of breaches. Also, with such a large dataset, ensuring accurate insights and avoiding misinterpretation become paramount.

Emerging Trends and Future Outlook

The horizon of Big Data continues to expand. With the Internet of Things (IoT) propelling us forward, more devices than ever are feeding into this data reservoir. The potential applications are vast—be it predicting market shifts, enhancing healthcare outcomes, or crafting highly personalized customer experiences. As we increasingly lean on Big Data, the onus of ethical and responsible data use also intensifies.

Module 5 Closing

We finished this module about the bast domain of data, where we recognize the emergence of a world where decisions are no longer gut-driven but are shaped and molded by the unwavering authority of data.

The synthesis, visualization, and strategic utilization of data have become imperatives in the modern digital era, playing a pivotal role in scripting success stories in the contemporary business landscape.

What do we take from all this?

Data's Impactful Narration: The artful application of Data Analytics delivers impactful narratives, carving out actions and strategic decisions from the raw, seemingly chaotic data, showcasing a powerful blend of art and science.

Structural Coherence in Data Management: MySQL brings forth structural coherence to data management, ensuring secure, organized, and effective data storage, which acts as an unshakable foundation for applications and data-driven strategies.

Visual Brilliance in Data Communication: Utilizing tools like Tableau and Looker, data transcends numeric expressions, morphing into comprehensible and striking visual narratives, thereby simplifying complex datasets into engaging stories.

Strategizing with Data-driven Intelligence: Business Intelligence isn't merely a concept but a practice, driving businesses to sculpt data-informed strategies and to navigate through the competitive market with a data-backed game plan.

Synthesizing and Structuring with Data Engineering: Through the lens of Data Science and Data Engineering, data becomes a meticulously crafted architecture, where streamlined data flow and insightful extractions pave the path for informed decision-making.

Unraveling the Enormity of Information: Big Data doesn't just refer to volume but speaks to the colossal potential hidden within vast datasets, waiting to unveil patterns and correlations that possess the power to shift paradigms and influence global trends.

All this doesn't come without a cost and our data it's a very vulnerable asset, so let's jump into the cybersecurity module!

Module 6 - Cybersecurity. Be prepared. Stay safe.

We've discovered many of the wonders of information technology and all the value they deliver to our personal and business life. But lurking below the surface are some digital dangers that can turn our use of technology into a nightmare. Welcome to the world of cybersecurity.

Cybersecurity isn't just for those mysterious hackers in dark rooms. No, it's for you, me, our friends who just set up her Instagram account or new App on the smartphone.

In this module, we'll demystify terms like "Data Encryption" and "VPN" and make them as relatable as your favorite sitcom. Ever wondered why you keep getting those pesky requests to enable "Two-factor Authentication" or puzzled over what "Ransomware" really means? We've got you!

Whether you're looking to secure your digital diary or ensure that only you can access your online knitting patterns, this module is here to help. Let's dive deep to understand and navigate the virtual threats, making sure you're protected in this ever-evolving digital landscape.

Chapter 44: Data Encryption

The Digital Lock and Key

Imagine you've written a secret note, but instead of hiding it under your pillow or handing it discreetly to a friend, you transform the text into a series of seemingly random characters. To the uninitiated, it looks like gibberish, but to those with the correct 'key', it's decipherable. Welcome to the world of Data Encryption.

Data Encryption is the practice of converting data into a code to prevent unauthorized access. In its encrypted form, data is unreadable without the proper decryption key. There are two primary types of encryption: symmetric, where the same key is used to both encrypt and decrypt the data, and asymmetric, where different keys are used for the encryption and decryption processes. This ensures that sensitive data, whether it's your online banking details, private messages, or company secrets, remains confidential and secure from prying eyes.

Practical Examples

Online Banking: Ever noticed that little padlock icon on your browser when you access your bank account online? That's encryption at work, safeguarding your account details and transactions.

Messaging Apps: Platforms like WhatsApp use end-to-end encryption. This means only you and the person you're messaging can read the texts. Not even the app provider can sneak a peek!

Online Shopping: When you enter your credit card details to buy those fabulous shoes or that shiny gadget, encryption ensures that prying eyes can't steal your financial information.

Potential Pitfalls

While encryption is like a fortress for data, it's not infallible. Some of the challenges include:

Weak Encryption Methods: Not all encryption methods are equal. Some can be easily broken into, kind of like using a flimsy lock on a treasure chest.

Malware: Certain malicious software can bypass or even break encryption, giving hackers access to your precious data.

Emerging Trends and Future Outlook

As technology progresses, so does the sophistication of cyberattacks. This means encryption methods must continually evolve. Quantum computing, a new frontier in tech, threatens to break many current encryption algorithms. However, on the flip side, it also promises to usher in an era of ultra-secure, quantum encryption. Additionally, as more devices get connected to the internet (think IoT), the demand for robust encryption techniques will only surge.

Remember, in the grand digital ocean, encryption is like that trusty life jacket, keeping your data safe from the lurking sharks. Swim on with confidence!

Chapter 45: SSO (Single Sign-On)
The Digital Bouncer of Your Online Club

Single Sign-On, commonly known as SSO, is like your golden ticket in Willy Wonka's digital chocolate factory. With just one set of credentials (username and password), you gain access to multiple applications or services. Instead of remembering a dozen passwords for different sites, SSO simplifies life by consolidating authentication.

More technically, SSO works by validating your identity with a central service. Once validated, it issues authentication tokens when you access other affiliated services. It's a bridge between unrelated websites, letting you traverse seamlessly without constantly re-entering your password.

Practical Examples

Corporate Environments: Ever noticed in office settings how you log into your computer and automatically have access to email, internal portals, and other tools? That's SSO doing its thing.

Google Suite: If you've logged into Gmail, you can effortlessly switch to Google Drive, YouTube, or Calendar without re-entering your credentials. Google knows you and rolls out the red carpet across its services.

Online Shopping: Some e-commerce platforms allow you to sign in via Facebook or Google. That's SSO in action, letting you skip the usual sign-up rigmarole.

Potential Pitfalls

SSO is convenient, but it's like putting all your eggs in one basket. This creates a Single Point of Failure: If a hacker gains access to your SSO credentials, they have the keys to multiple services. It's a jackpot for them.

Also there are privacy Concerns: Using third-party SSO services (like logging in via Facebook) can mean those platforms get a peek into your activities on other sites.

Emerging Trends and Future Outlook

The need for secure and user-friendly authentication is on the rise. As such, we might see more advanced SSO solutions that incorporate biometrics (like fingerprint or facial recognition). There's also a growing trend towards decentralized authentication, where users have more control over their identity data.

In the future, as online platforms proliferate, ensuring seamless, secure, and privacy-preserving SSO mechanisms will be paramount. After all, who wants to remember a zillion passwords in the digital age?

Chapter 46: 2FA (Two-factor Authentication)

The Double-Check of the Digital World

Remember those days when you'd double-lock your door before leaving for a vacation? Or when the bank teller asks for an additional ID just to be sure? That's the essence of 2FA in the virtual realm – an extra layer, a second nod, ensuring it's really you knocking. We've all been there: entering a password and thinking, "This should keep things safe, right?" But what if someone gets a hold of that precious password? Enter 2FA.

Two-factor Authentication, abbreviated as 2FA, is a security measure that requires two types of identification before granting access. The first factor? Usually something you know, like a password. The second? It could be something you have (like a phone or hardware token) or something you inherently are (fingerprint or retina scan).

Practical Examples

Online Banking: After entering the password, your bank might send an SMS with a code. Only after entering this code can you access your account.

Social Media: Ever tried logging into Facebook from a new device? They will ask for a verification code sent to your registered email.

Potential Pitfalls

2FA is like a digital fortress, but every fortress has its vulnerabilities:

Reliance on Devices: If you're using your phone as the second authentication factor and it's lost, you might be locked out of your accounts.

Phishing Threats: Crafty hackers can dupe users into providing both the password and the 2FA code, gaining access.

Inconvenience: Sometimes, that extra step feels tedious, especially if you're in a rush.

Emerging Trends and Future Outlook

With cyber threats growing more sophisticated, 2FA is quickly evolving. We're witnessing a shift towards 'adaptive' authentication, where the system decides the level of verification based on user behavior. Also, as biometric technology improves, fingers and faces might become our primary 2FA tools.

In the horizon, a blend of AI, behavior patterns, and biometrics could redefine 2FA, making security both effortless and robust. Imagine a future where your devices just "know" it's you, no codes needed.

Chapter 47: VPN (Virtual private Network)

The Invisible Cloak of the Digital World

Ever wanted a secret tunnel that lets you bypass that pesky "content not available in your region" message? Welcome to the magic of VPNs, where your digital footprints turn into whispers. Imagine you're sending a top-secret love letter through a crowded room. You don't want the snoopy folks to read it. So, you use a secret tunnel known only to you and your beloved. That's a VPN for you, but for your online activities.

A Virtual Private Network (VPN) is a technology that creates a secure, encrypted connection between your device and the internet. It masks your IP address, making your online actions almost untraceable. With VPN, your data travels through a secure tunnel, keeping eavesdroppers and cybercriminals at bay.

Practical Examples

Streaming Shows: Want to watch that exclusive British detective show but live in Australia? A VPN can change your location, giving you access.

Safe Public Wi-Fi: Using the free Wi-Fi at the airport? VPNs ensure your data remains encrypted, safe from prying eyes.

Private Browsing: If you don't fancy advertisers tracking every site you visit, a VPN is your ally, making your browsing truly private.

Potential Pitfalls

Wearing the cloak of VPN does come with its share of hitches:
Speed Drops: Since your data is taking the scenic route via a VPN server, sometimes it slows down a bit.
Not All VPNs are Equal: Some might log your activities, defeating the very purpose of privacy.
Compatibility Issues: Not all devices and websites are VPN-friendly. Some streaming services, for instance, block VPN users.

Emerging Trends and Future Outlook

The VPN world is gearing up for some exciting times. As privacy concerns skyrocket, decentralized VPNs, powered by blockchain, are on the rise, promising even more anonymity. And as AI enters the scene, we can expect VPNs that auto-adjust based on our needs, offering optimum speed and security.

In the not-so-distant future, VPN might transition from being an option to a default setting, a staple in our quest for a safer digital existence.

Chapter 48: Phishing

The digital fraudulent impersonation

Remember those fairy tales where a witch offers a poisoned apple, and the unsuspecting protagonist takes a bite? Well, in the digital world, there's no apple, but there sure are a lot of deceptive emails and links waiting for a bite. Welcome to the realm of phishing, where cyber tricksters await with baited intentions.

Phishing is a form of cyber-attack where attackers disguise themselves as trustworthy entities to trick victims into revealing sensitive information. This could be passwords, credit card numbers, or other personal data. By using a mix of psychological manipulation and technical tricks, phishers lure their victims into their traps.

Practical Examples

The Lottery Win: An email claims you've won a vast sum of money, but first, they need some "verification" details. Spoiler: There's no jackpot.

Tech Support Scams: A pop-up warning claims your computer is infected and you need to call a number or download software. It's all smoke and mirrors.

Fake Invoices: You receive an email with an invoice for a service you never purchased, but clicking on it could unleash malware or solicit personal details.

Potential Pitfalls

Phishing isn't just about deceptive emails:

Spear Phishing: This is a more targeted form of phishing, where attackers customize their baits based on their knowledge of the victim.

Vishing: Phishing via phone calls. Yes, those unsolicited calls claiming they're from tech support? Classic vishing.

Phishing Sites: Websites that mimic legitimate sites to steal data. They might look genuine, but a closer look at the URL often reveals the deception.

Emerging Trends and Future Outlook

Phishing is evolving, becoming more sophisticated with time. With the rise of AI, we're seeing machine-generated phishing emails that are eerily convincing. There's also "Deepfake Phishing", where attackers use manipulated audio or video to deceive their victims.

However, on the brighter side, innovations in authentication processes, AI-driven security systems, and user education are making strides to combat these threats. Soon, with combined human vigilance and tech prowess, we might just make phishing a thing of the past.

Chapter 49: Ransomware
When Your Data Gets Held Hostage

Picture this: You're having a relaxing Sunday morning, sipping on your coffee, and decide to check your computer. Instead of the usual welcome screen, there's a sinister message: "Your files are encrypted. Pay up, or lose them forever." This is ransomware.

Ransomware is a type of malicious software designed to block access to a computer system or files until a sum of money, or 'ransom', is paid. Once ransomware gets into a system, it encrypts the victim's files, making them inaccessible. The attacker then demands payment, typically in cryptocurrency due to its anonymity, to provide the decryption key.

Practical Examples

Local City's Systems Held Hostage: a city's public service systems gets infected. Essential services at a standstill, the city might be forced to pay the ransom.

Personal Photo Leak Threat: A user's personal computer gets infected, and the attacker threatens to leak sensitive photos or documents unless paid. It's personal and deeply violating.

Potential Pitfalls

While paying the ransom might seem like the quickest way out, it's fraught with risks:

No Guarantee of Decryption: After payment, attackers might not provide the decryption key, leaving victims both penniless and data-less.

Repeat Targeting: Paying once might mark you as an easy target, leading to repeat attacks.

Funding Cybercrime: Paying the ransom directly contributes to the flourishing of the cybercriminal ecosystem.

Emerging Trends and Future Outlook

Ransomware is getting craftier. We're seeing an alarming rise in "double extortion" schemes. Here, attackers not only encrypt data but threaten to release it publicly, increasing the pressure to pay. Moreover, with the increasing number of IoT devices, there's a potential for ransomware attacks on unconventional devices – think smart fridges or wearables.

On the optimistic front, global collaboration, improved cybersecurity measures, and public awareness campaigns are aiding in the fight against these cyber threats. In the future, with fortified defenses, we might see a decline in successful ransomware attacks.

Module 6 Closing

Cybersecurity module has unveiled the profound depth and criticality of securing data and maintaining privacy in the digital era.

Let's review the key insights around the concepts that draw the preventative and responsive measures available to secure data and safeguard users in the digital world.

Imperative of Encryption: Data Encryption protects information by converting it into a ciphered format, rendering it unreadable to unauthorized entities and ensuring its safety during transmission and storage.

Simplifying Secure Access: SSO, as discussed in Chapter 45, allows for secure and seamless access across multiple applications with a single set of credentials, balancing user experience and security.

Enhancing Security Layers: 2FA implements an extra layer of security by requiring two distinct forms of identification, creating a rigorous defense against unauthorized access.

Securing Data Transmission: VPNs establish a secure internet connection by encrypting data transmissions, crafting a secure tunnel that guards data from potential interceptors.

Guarding Against Deceptive Tactics: Phishing employs deceptive tactics to trick users into revealing sensitive information, underscoring the essential role of user awareness and vigilance.

Mitigating Data Hostage Situations: Ransomware exemplifies a critical cybersecurity threat by holding user data hostage, underscoring the importance of robust security, and recovery strategies.

Feeling safe now? Let's market yourself then!

Module 7 - Digital Marketing. It's not just social media.

Ever wondered how that pair of shoes you casually glanced at online seems to follow you across every website, email, and even on your social media? Or how certain companies seem to "get you" with their content, making you feel like they've been reading your diary? They are all-in digital marketing.

Digital marketing It's more than just ads and emails. It's a digital opera of understanding customers, making connections, and fostering relationships in the vast, ever-changing online space. With the right steps, it transforms casual browsers into loyal customers and sometimes even ardent brand advocates.

In this module, we'll venture into this intricate dance floor, learning the steps from acquisition to retention, diving deep into the metrics that matter (like CAC and Churn), and exploring tools that marketers wield (like SEO and SEM). We'll understand how landing pages work and why inbound marketing might be the instrument in the house.

The digital marketing concert is about to start, and you're on the guest list!

Chapter 50: Acquisition and Retention
Attract, Keep, Repeat

The Two Pillars of Growth: Imagine setting up a shop. You'd want people to come in, browse, and buy something, right? But it's not just about getting them through the door once. Ideally, you'd want them to come back, again and again. In the digital age, this translates to acquisition and retention.

Acquisition refers to the initial stage of gaining new users or customers. Think of it as the first impression, the initial spark. It could be through an ad, a referral, social media, or even word of mouth. The methods are many, but the goal remains the same: get 'em on board.

Retention, on the other hand, is about keeping that spark alive. It's ensuring that users or customers continue to engage with a brand or product over time. Retention strategies might involve personalized emails, loyalty programs, or even new product features that cater to user feedback.

Practical Examples

Subscription Boxes: Companies offer enticing initial discounts to acquire new subscribers. They then provide exclusive perks or quality products to retain these subscribers month after month.

Streaming Platforms: Platforms like Netflix acquire users by offering unique shows or limited-time trials. To retain viewers, they constantly update their content library and provide personalized recommendations.

Loyalty Programs: Many coffee shops or stores offer loyalty cards. Buy nine coffees, get the tenth free. This is a retention strategy, ensuring that customers choose them repeatedly.

Potential Pitfalls

Focusing too much on acquisition and neglecting retention can be costly. It's a mistake to think that once a user is acquired, the job is done. Without proper engagement and value addition, churn rates (people leaving or stopping using a service) can skyrocket. Similarly, solely concentrating on retention without fresh acquisition can stagnant growth.

Emerging Trends and Future Outlook

As competition in the digital space intensifies, businesses are investing more in understanding user behavior. Predictive analytics, personalized engagement strategies, and more integrated user experiences are paving the way. The future likely holds a more balanced and data-driven approach to both acquisition and retention, ensuring businesses can grow while keeping their foundational user base engaged and satisfied.

Chapter 51: CAC and Churn

CAC and Churn: Decoding the Cost of Wooing and Losing

In the world of business, especially when digital platforms are involved, two crucial metrics often dictate success: CAC (Customer Acquisition Cost) and churn.

CAC stands for Customer Acquisition Cost. Simply put, it's the total cost of convincing a potential customer to buy a product or service. This can include advertising costs, promotional expenses, and even the cost of the sales team. It's a reflection of how efficiently a business can attract new customers. The lower the CAC, the better.

Churn, on the flip side, measures how many customers or subscribers stop using a product or service over a particular period. It's often expressed as a percentage and represents the leak in your bucket. The lower the churn rate, the better the retention of customers.

Practical Examples

Streaming Services: If a streaming service spends $1 million on advertising in a month and gains 50,000 new subscribers, its CAC is $20. However, if 5,000 of those new subscribers cancel the next month, they have a 10% churn rate.

Mobile Apps: An app might spend on ads to attract new users. If they acquire 1,000 users at a cost of $5,000, their CAC is $5. But, if 200 of those users uninstall the app within a month, the churn rate stands at 20%.

Potential Pitfalls

High CAC and high churn can be a deadly combination for businesses. Spending a lot to acquire customers who then leave in droves isn't sustainable. On the other hand, very low CAC might mean you're not investing enough in growth, while low churn without fresh acquisition can lead to stagnation.

Emerging Trends and Future Outlook

As businesses lean more into analytics, tools predicting churn based on user behavior patterns are gaining traction. This allows companies to intervene proactively, maybe with special offers or features, before a user decides to leave. Meanwhile, organic acquisition methods, like content marketing, are being explored to reduce CAC.

Understanding the dance between CAC and churn helps businesses craft strategies that are cost-effective and customer-centric. After all, it's not just about getting them to the party; it's ensuring they stay for the long haul.

Chapter 52: Landing Page

Your Digital First Impression

Have you ever clicked on an advertisement or a link, expecting to find more about a product, service, or event, and landed on a specifically designed page? That's a landing page for you.

A landing page is a standalone web page, distinct from your main website, created specifically for marketing or advertising campaigns. Its primary goal is to convert visitors into leads or customers. Whether it's to sign up for a newsletter, register for a webinar, or purchase a product, a landing page is optimized to prompt the visitor to take a specific action.

The design, content, and call-to-action (CTA) of a landing page are crucial. Unlike other web pages that might have various goals or messages, a landing page is laser-focused on one action.

Practical Examples

Event Registration: An organization promoting an upcoming webinar might create a landing page with details about the topics, speakers, and a form to register for the event.

Product Launch: A tech company unveiling a new gadget might use a landing page to highlight its features, show a flashy promo video, and have a pre-order button.

Newsletter Signup: A blogger or news site could use a landing page to encourage readers to sign up for weekly updates or premium content.

Potential Pitfalls

One of the most common mistakes is overloading the landing page with too much information, making it cluttered and overwhelming. Another pitfall is not having a clear or compelling CTA, leading to confusion or a lack of interest from the visitor.

Emerging Trends and Future Outlook

Personalization is the buzzword. Modern landing pages are leaning towards offering tailored experiences. Tools are being developed that adjust landing page content based on the user's past behavior, demographics, or source of the visit. Additionally, with the rise of mobile browsing, optimizing landing pages for mobile devices is paramount.

A landing page is your digital first impression. And just like in real life, you've got a limited window to dazzle and captivate. Done right, it can be the difference between a fleeting visit and a long-term relationship.

Chapter 53: SEO
Making Sure Google Has a Crush on You

You might've often wondered, how do some websites always seem to be at the top of your search results? It's like magic, right? Not quite – it's all thanks to SEO.

Search Engine Optimization (SEO) is the practice of optimizing your online content to increase its visibility in search engines for relevant searches. The ultimate goal? To be at the top of the search results, or as close to it as possible, without paying for ads.

SEO involves understanding what people are searching for, the words they're using, and the type of content they wish to consume. With this knowledge, you can produce content that appeals to search engines and users alike.

Practical Examples

Keyword Integration: A local bakery might include terms like "best cherry pie in [city name]" in its web content, ensuring locals find them when they search for that delicious treat.

Link Building: A tech blogger writes a detailed review of a new phone, which gets linked by a popular tech news site, boosting the blogger's website authority and search rank.

Mobile Optimization: An e-commerce store ensures its website is responsive, so it appears higher in searches made from mobile devices.

Potential Pitfalls

While SEO can work wonders, it's not without pitfalls. Overstuffing your content with keywords (known as "keyword stuffing") can backfire and lead to search engine penalties. Also, focusing solely on search engines and neglecting the actual human readers can result in lackluster content that doesn't truly engage.

Emerging Trends and Future Outlook

Voice search is revolutionizing SEO. As more people use voice-activated devices, the nature of search queries becomes more conversational. Adapting to this trend requires a nuanced approach. Additionally, the rise of video content means optimizing for platforms like YouTube is now a significant part of SEO strategy.

Being Google's favorite isn't about deception but about providing valuable, genuine content that meets users' needs. It's an ongoing dance, where staying in step with the latest SEO trends ensures you remain in the spotlight.

Chapter 54: SEM (Search Engine Marketing)
Investing in Digital Real Estate

If SEO is the art of organically climbing to the top of search results, SEM is like paying for a VIP ticket to get you there quicker.

Search Engine Marketing (SEM) is a digital marketing strategy that involves promoting your website by increasing its visibility in search engine results pages primarily through paid advertising. Think of it as buying ad space on Google's first page.

While SEO focuses on earning traffic through unpaid or free listings, SEM is all about buying traffic through paid search listings. Every time someone clicks on your ad, you pay a fee, hence the commonly used term: "pay-per-click" (PPC) advertising.

Practical Examples

Pay-Per-Click (PPC) Campaigns: A shoe store launches a PPC campaign on Google Ads. Every time a user clicks on their ad after searching for "running shoes," the store pays a set fee.

Product Listing Ads (PLA): An online electronics store displays its products directly in search results with images, prices, and descriptions, enticing users to click.

Local Search Ads: A newly-opened cafe uses local search ads to appear prominently when nearby users search for "cafes near me."

Potential Pitfalls

SEM requires a budget, and if not managed properly, costs can spiral. Moreover, without a well-optimized landing page, high click rates won't necessarily translate to conversions. It's crucial to target the right keywords; otherwise, you might attract traffic that's not genuinely interested in what you offer.

Emerging Trends and Future Outlook

With advancements in artificial intelligence, SEM platforms are becoming more sophisticated in targeting and bid strategies. Ad personalization is also evolving, allowing businesses to craft ads tailored to individual users' habits and preferences. The growth of voice search and smart devices also points towards a future where SEM strategies will expand beyond traditional text-based search.

Paying for a prime spot can be a game-changer, but like any investment, SEM requires strategy, monitoring, and regular adjustments to ensure you're getting bang for your buck.

Chapter 55: Email marketing
Not Your Regular Inbox Invasion

Who hasn't experienced the excitement of getting a fresh email, only to find out it's yet another promotional offer? Yet, when done right, email marketing is the charming prince in the digital kingdom, turning casual browsers into devoted customers.

Email Marketing is the art and science of sending targeted messages to a group of people via email. It's not about bombarding inboxes but delivering value: from newsletters to promotions, product announcements, and more.

This strategy aims to foster relationships, keep your brand on top of the mind, and ultimately drive sales. It's personal, direct, and when used effectively, can have one of the highest return on investments in the digital marketing world.

Practical Examples

Newsletters: A lifestyle blogger sends out a monthly newsletter, updating subscribers on recent posts, personal anecdotes, and recommended products.

Promotional Campaigns: A clothing brand sends exclusive discount codes to its email subscribers during holiday seasons.

Potential Pitfalls

Sending too many emails or irrelevant content can lead to subscribers feeling overwhelmed and hitting the "unsubscribe" button. Poorly designed emails, which don't render well on mobile devices or aren't personalized, can also fall flat. Furthermore, not adhering to regulations like the General Data Protection Regulation (GDPR) can result in hefty penalties for businesses.

Emerging Trends and Future Outlook

The world of email marketing is evolving to become even more personalized and interactive. With AI-driven insights, brands can now predict what content a user might engage with. Also, interactive emails with embedded videos, polls, and clickable elements are making inroads. As inboxes become smarter, brands need to up their email game, ensuring every communication adds value, not noise.

In a world saturated with fleeting social media updates, email marketing stands as a stalwart, ensuring a direct line to your audience's digital heart.

Chapter 56: Inbound Marketing
The art of attraction

Remember the thrill of a treasure hunt? Inbound marketing is a bit like that. Instead of aggressively pursuing customers, you create valuable content that lures them towards your brand, making them come to you.

Inbound marketing focuses on creating content tailored to potential customers' needs and interests, making it more likely they'll find you during their own research.

The idea is to offer insights, solutions, and resources that help them at different stages of their buying journey. From blog posts and eBooks to webinars and social media content, the aim is to engage, delight, and, eventually, convert visitors into loyal customers.

Practical Examples

Educational Webinars: A software company hosts webinars, offering solutions and tutorials on industry-specific challenges, turning casual viewers into potential leads.

SEO-Optimized Blog Posts: A health and wellness website publishes articles on trending topics like "Keto Diet Benefits," drawing organic traffic from search engine users.

Interactive Quizzes: A skincare brand offers a "Find Your Skin Type" quiz, engaging visitors, and providing personalized product recommendations based on results.

Potential Pitfalls

The biggest challenge in inbound marketing is creating content that genuinely resonates and offers value. It's a time-intensive approach, and brands can get discouraged if they don't see immediate results. Moreover, without a comprehensive strategy, efforts can scatter, missing the mark in genuinely attracting and converting potential customers.

Emerging Trends and Future Outlook

With the information overload in the digital world, the future of inbound marketing hinges on hyper-personalization and interactivity. AI-driven content recommendations, virtual reality experiences, and more immersive storytelling methods are set to redefine how brands pull audiences into their orbit.

Inbound marketing is like hosting a party where every guest feels personally invited and leaves with a gift. Done right, it's not just marketing; it's an experience.

Module 7 Closing

In this module, each chapter provided lenses through which to view the multifaceted aspects of attracting, converting, and retaining customers in the digital space.

Crafting, not just campaigns, but journeys, relationships, and experiences in the digital domain has become pivotal. Let's review the main takeaways.

Beyond Gaining and Keeping: Acquisition and Retention are not mere stages but an intricate dance of attracting and holistically integrating customers into a brand's narrative, cultivating not just consumers but advocates through value, engagement, and experience.

Metrics that Reveal and Direct: CAC and Churn don't just quantify costs and losses but guide strategic direction, revealing underlying narratives about customer value, loyalty, and revealing paths to financially sustainable customer relationship dynamics.

Entrances Crafted with Intent: Landing Pages serve not just as digital doorways but strategic funnels that curate a visitor's journey, meticulously guiding them from curiosity to conversion through precise design and messaging.

Visibility with Value: SEO is more than ranking, it's more the art and science of crafting visibility that is rooted in genuine value, ensuring that digital presences are not just seen but resonate and are relevant to seekers.

Strategic Digital Presence: SEM extends beyond paid advertising, emerging as a nuanced strategy that meticulously places a brand in a searcher's path, blending visibility with strategic targeting to garner not just clicks but connections.

Personalized Digital Correspondence: Email Marketing transcends sending messages, emerging as a platform for curating personalized, value-rich dialogues that nurture, inform, and convert receivers into engaged customers and brand advocates.

Magnetic Marketing: Inbound Marketing isn't simply a tactic but a philosophy that magnetizes a brand, crafting experiences, content, and value that naturally draw in audiences, nurturing them from interest to advocacy.

You are just 3 modules ahead to become an expert. Let's keep going!

Module 8 - Enterprise tools. The backstage of businesses.

Ever browsed through an online store, marveling at the smooth navigation, or received an email precisely when your favorite store was having a sale? Did you ever wonder, "How do they manage all this? The answer is Enterprise Tools.

Enterprise tools, in essence, are the heavy-duty machinery behind the sleek, polished curtain of businesses. From the Operating System (OS), which serves as the backbone, providing an environment where software applications can shine, to Customer Relationship Management (CRM) tools that remember your birthday and ERPs that control every single operation. These tools collectively create an intricate ballet that orchestrates how businesses interact with us, their audience.

How these tools do the relentless work in streamlining, organizing, and automating a plethora of business processes is what this module is all about.

Let's uncover it!

Chapter 57: OS (Operating System)

The Unsung Hero of Your Daily Digital Adventures

Have you ever wondered how you can seamlessly switch between apps, browse files, or customize your device settings? This magic is orchestrated by an Operating System or OS for short. Think of it as the middleman, communicating between the software applications you use and the physical hardware of your computer or smartphone.

In technical terms, the OS is system software that manages computer hardware and provides various services for computer programs. It acts as an intermediary between users and the computer hardware. The OS controls and coordinates the use of the hardware amongst the computer's various types of software and the users. It manages memory, processes, and all of its software and hardware. It also allows us to communicate with the computer without knowing how to speak the computer's language.

Practical Examples

Computers OS - Windows and Mac: When it comes to desktop computers and laptops, Windows and macOS are like the Coca-Cola and Pepsi of the OS world. Windows, with its versatile and user-friendly interface, has been a favorite among businesses and personal users alike. On the other side, macOS, with its sleek design and robust security, has carved out its niche, particularly among creative professionals.

Mobile OS - iOS and Android: iOS and Android steer the ship in the vast ocean of mobile technology. iOS, with its seamless operation and premium aura, has been a staple among the elite smartphone users, while Android has conquered a vast territory thanks to its adaptability and extensive device range, from budget-friendly to premium devices.

Other OS - Linux and Unix: Beyond the conventional, there's Linux and Unix, the unsung heroes often reserved for more technical applications. Linux is celebrated in the tech world for its stability and security, used extensively for servers and development environments. Meanwhile, Unix, with its powerful features, is commonly utilized in enterprises and data centers, ensuring the digital world stays in rhythm.

Potential Pitfalls

The OS is not exempt from challenges. Selecting an OS that doesn't align with your software needs can lead to compatibility nightmares. Furthermore, they are not impervious to threats; they require regular updates to patch vulnerabilities and ensure optimal performance and security.

Emerging Trends and Future Outlook

In our futuristic lens, the OS will evolve, embracing more integrative and adaptive functionalities. Imagine an OS that learns from your behaviors and customizes your digital environment to enhance productivity and user experience. Moreover, with the advent of quantum computing and AI, future OSs will need to transcend current functionalities, offering support for new computing paradigms, and ensuring a secure, stable, and scalable environment in the ever-expanding digital cosmos.

Chapter 58: CRM (Customer Relationship Management)

The maestro orchestrating the symphony of client relationships.

Imagine having a magic book that detailed everything about your friends—their birthdays, favorite restaurants, and even the last time you hung out. Now, translate this to a business context, and you have CRM. A Customer Relationship Management (CRM) system is a powerful tool that helps businesses organize, analyze, and utilize their customer data.

Customer Relationship Management (CRM) software is a tool that manages a company's interactions with current and future customers. It uses data analysis about customers' history with a company to improve business relationships, specifically focusing on customer retention and ultimately driving sales growth. A CRM system helps companies stay connected to customers, streamline processes, and improve profitability by organizing and analyzing customer interactions throughout the customer lifecycle.

Practical Examples

Salesforce: The Heavyweight Champ of CRM: Dominating the CRM market, Salesforce is renowned for its comprehensive, cloud-based tools, providing solutions that aid businesses in tracking customer activities, market to customers, and many more functionalities.

HubSpot: The Darling of Inbound Marketing: A favorite, especially among SMEs, HubSpot integrates marketing, sales, and service software that assists businesses to attract visitors, convert leads, and close customers.

Zoho CRM: The Underdog Making Waves: Catering to small and medium-sized businesses, Zoho CRM offers solutions that refine customer services, enhance marketing strategies, and enrich the customer journey, all while being pocket-friendly.

Potential Pitfalls

One can imagine how a symphony could turn dissonant if the conductor isn't adept. Similarly, the misuse or poor management of a CRM system can spiral into a cacophony of mismanaged data, poor customer service, and squandered leads. Implementing a CRM system that is overly complex for the needs of the business, or conversely, one that lacks required functionalities, can be as catastrophic as a maestro missing a beat during a concert. Furthermore, inadequate training of staff and inconsistent use of the system can derail the promising journey CRM has to offer.

Emerging Trends and Future Outlook

The encore to the CRM symphony appears to be equally enticing. AI and machine learning are being woven into CRM systems, enabling predictive analytics and smarter customer insights. The future might unveil a CRM that not only manages customer relationships but also anticipates their needs, creating a melody that continually adapts and evolves, ensuring the music of customer satisfaction plays on seamlessly.

Chapter 59: ERP (Enterprise Resource Planning)
Steer the enterprise ship in the corporate ocean.

Picture this: A bustling seaport, where goods are loaded and unloaded, ships come in and out, and every item must be tracked and managed to ensure smooth sailing of operations. Metaphorically speaking, this seaport resembles an enterprise, and the Enterprise Resource Planning (ERP) system is its adept harbor master, ensuring each crate (data) is precisely where it should be. ERPs meticulously map out the route, ensuring that all departments within the organization are harmoniously sailing toward their common goal: seamless operation and profitability.

ERP is a type of software that organizations use to manage their day-to-day activities. The system helps in managing business processes, which can be centralized and regularly assessed to ensure that everything is in shipshape. This is achieved through the collection, storage, management, and interpretation of data from various business activities, including supply chain management, procurement, manufacturing, services delivery, project management, financial management, inventory management, order processing, and more.

Practical Examples

SAP ERP: One of the giants in the ERP market, SAP offers solutions that manage business operations and customer relations smoothly and cohesively, akin to a massive freighter smoothly navigating through the busiest ports.

Oracle ERP Cloud: Offering cloud-based ERP solutions, Oracle propels businesses with robust and comprehensive tools to navigate through the stormy seas of data management and financial planning with agility and precision.

Microsoft Dynamics 365: Microsoft's ERP solution, with its extensive and adaptable functionalities, assists businesses in managing their finance, operations, and customer support.

Potential Pitfalls

Navigating through the vast ocean of enterprise data and operations without any mishaps requires a sturdy and reliable ERP system. However, a myriad of challenges like high costs, complex implementations, and the potential resistance from employees due to the change in work processes can be akin to the perilous icebergs, ready to rip through the vessel of efficient management. Moreover, a lack of customization and scalability in your chosen ERP system can hinder the growth of a business, acting as an anchor preventing it from sailing towards its goals.

Emerging Trends and Future Outlook

With the incorporation of AI and IoT, ERPs are evolving into intelligent systems capable of making data-driven decisions and providing insightful analytics. Moreover, with cloud computing steering the helm, ERP systems are becoming more accessible, scalable, and secure, ensuring enterprises, whether large or small, can navigate through the global market's turbulent waves with confidence and competence.

Chapter 60: CMS (Content Management System)
Finding the digital filing cabinet

It's a universal truth: Nobody loves a cluttered, chaotic filing cabinet. Imagine, if you will, wading through mountains of papers to find that one crucial document. Stressful, isn't it? Now, imagine a magical filing cabinet that not only organizes all your documents efficiently but also allows you to create, manage, and modify content without the need to dive into the intricacies of coding. This, in essence, is the work of a Content Management System (CMS).

CMS is software that helps users create, manage, and modify content on a website without the need for specialized technical knowledge. In simpler terms, it takes the brain-ache out of managing digital content, giving users the freedom to focus on the message, not the medium. CMS platforms provide a centralized repository where businesses, bloggers, and other creators can manage their content in one space, ensuring consistency and efficiency.

Practical Examples

WordPress: Known for its user-friendly interface and a vast array of plugins, WordPress is a beloved CMS among bloggers and businesses, providing flexible options for all sorts of web content creation and management.

Joomla!: Providing extensive functionalities and being highly customizable, Joomla! offers an efficient way for developers and non-developers alike to mold their content creation environment to their precise needs.

Shopify: Predominantly catering to e-commerce platforms, Shopify simplifies online store management, enabling users to focus on their products and customers instead of getting bogged down with web development intricacies.

Potential Pitfalls

But beware, the seemingly calm seas of CMS have their share of storms. There's the risk of choosing a CMS that is too complex for your team's technical expertise, leading to underutilization of its features or poor content management. Also, scalability can become an issue. Some CMS platforms may not be able to keep up with the growing volume and complexity of content, and switching platforms can be a cumbersome process.

Emerging Trends and Future Outlook

As we sail into the future, CMSs are adapting to the shifting winds of digital evolution. With the rise of omnichannel marketing, CMS platforms are evolving to manage and disseminate content across various channels seamlessly. Also, the application of Artificial Intelligence in CMS, such as chatbots and voice search optimization, and the integration of blockchain for secure and transparent content management, herald a future where CMS platforms will not just manage content but offer intelligent, secure, and multi-faceted digital experiences.

Chapter 61: PIM (Product Information Management)

Bridging the Gap Between Products and Customers

You stroll into a warehouse store ready to get everything for your house renovation. But uh-oh, it's a maelstrom of products with no signs, no order, and no assistance. You're lost in a sea of products with no idea where your desired items are. In the digital world, this chaos is curtailed by a system known as Product Information Management (PIM).

A PIM system is like the ultimate superstore guide, ensuring that all product data is stored, organized, and utilized effectively across all channels. It's not just a digital storage room; it's an intelligent tool that consolidates product information, ensuring consistency and accuracy, and smartly distributing it wherever it's needed, whether that's an e-commerce website, print catalog, or any other channel.

Practical Examples

Car Manufacturers: Picture brands like Tesla or BMW using PIM systems to manage intricate details of each model – everything from tech specifications, color options, pricing, and available upgrades, ensuring consistency across all marketing and sales channels.

Online Fashion Retailers: Imagine Zara, managing thousands of clothing items, accessories, and beauty products, ensuring every size, color variant, and style is accurately represented and updated in real-time across various platforms.

Electronic Superstores: Think of Best Buy, juggling numerous electronic items, keeping track of evolving tech specs, pricing, and vendor information, ensuring that customers always have access to the latest and most accurate product data.

Potential Pitfalls

It's not all smooth sailing with PIM. Challenges might sprout in the form of data quality issues and consistency in data management, especially if information sourced from various vendors lacks standardization. Moreover, implementing a PIM system requires considerable upfront investment and staff training to harness its full potential – it's a journey that needs strategic planning and execution.

Emerging Trends and Future Outlook

Peering into the future, PIM systems are set to evolve with richer functionalities, embracing augmented reality to provide immersive product visualizations and employing AI to automate data management and enhance customer personalization. The convergence of PIM with Internet of Things (IoT) also heralds a future where product data will be interlinked with smart devices, providing a seamless, intelligent, and highly personalized user experience.

Chapter 62: BPA (Business Process Automation)
Automating Success or Stress?

Imagine a workplace where routine tasks like scheduling, data entry, and email responses are magically taken care of, leaving you to sip on your coffee and focus on strategic projects. That's what Business Process Automation (BPA)will do for you. BPA is taking care of repetitive tasks automatically so businesses can optimize their operations.

BPA is all about utilizing technology to perform complex business processes and functions automatically, reducing manual effort, minimizing errors, and enhancing efficiency. It's the invisible cogs and wheels in an enterprise machinery, ensuring that daily operations, from the mundane to the critical, operate smoothly without necessitating constant human intervention.

Practical Examples

Automated Customer Service: Chatbots in customer service platforms, like those deployed by many e-commerce websites, handle FAQs and basic customer queries round the clock, ensuring immediate response at any hour.

Invoice Processing: Financial software in various firms automatically generates and sends invoices to clients, reduces manual work, and ensures timely billing and payment cycles.

Social Media Management: Tools like Hootsuite allow marketers to schedule posts across multiple social media platforms in one go, ensuring consistency in engagement without the need to manually post content regularly.

Potential Pitfalls

But let's pump the brakes for a moment! Implementing BPA isn't a stroll through the park. It involves thorough analysis and understanding of existing processes, and not all tasks are suitable for automation. Plus, improper implementation can lead to complexities and may unintentionally extend processes rather than streamline them. Also, there's the challenge of ensuring that the human workforce smoothly transitions and adapts to an automated environment, mastering new tools without feeling marginalized.

Emerging Trends and Future Outlook

Gazing into the crystal ball, BPA is on a steadfast journey towards more intelligent and adaptive systems. The incorporation of AI and machine learning is enabling BPA tools to make data-driven decisions and provide insights that can further streamline operations. Moreover, as companies increasingly shift towards remote working, BPA will play a pivotal role in ensuring that decentralized operations remain cohesive, consistent, and efficient.

Module 8 Closing

We are done on Module 8, let's take a brief moment to look at the key insights around Enterprise tools..

Unseen Facilitators: OS function silently in the background, yet they are paramount in orchestrating the harmony between hardware and software, defining the user-computer interaction and ensuring the systematic and seamless operation of devices and applications.

Nurturing Relationships Digitally: CRM systems embody more than tools; they act as digital ecosystems that nurture and fortify customer relationships, driving targeted engagements, retaining valuable connections, and transforming data into actionable customer-centric strategies.

Unified Enterprise Operations: ERP goes beyond a planning tool, forming a unified, data-driven backbone that integrates diverse organizational functions into a coherent, interconnected, and real-time operational entity, thereby enhancing strategic alignment and decision-making.

Digitizing Content Management: CMS are not just platforms but catalysts that democratize digital content creation, management, and publication, breaking down technical barriers and enabling expressive, agile, and scalable digital presences.

Centrally Orchestrating Product Information: PIM isn't merely a tool but a central orchestrator of product data, ensuring consistency, accuracy, and comprehensive management of product information across myriad channels.

Automating Success: BPA is not simply about automating tasks but about strategically enhancing, streamlining, and optimizing business processes through intelligent automation, driving efficiency, reducing errors, and enabling scalability.

Navigating through the digital scaffolding that supports and optimizes various business operations, from backend operations, customer relations, to data management, the importance of integrating digital tools to streamline, automate, and optimize business operations becomes increasingly evident.

Now you are ready to be a business opera maestro.

Module 9 - Fintech. Money in the age of technology.

Let's dive into Fintech, where finance and technology dance in a complex, yet enchanting duet. This module promises a kaleidoscope of concepts, from the enigmatic world of cryptocurrencies to the democratic ecosystem of crowdfunding.

Technological innovations are not just accelerating but also reshaping the financial sector, Fintech emerges as the protagonist, enabling transactions, investments, and financial management to be -as proponents say- more accessible, faster, and often, more secure.

We'll plunge into the depths of Cryptocurrency, exploring digital or virtual assets used as a medium of exchange, unpack the famed Bitcoin, know about distributed finances as well as the benefits of crowdfunding.

Navigating towards IPOs, we'll demystify the how's and why's of Initial Public Offerings. Lastly, we delve into the realm of Smart Contracts, exploring self-executing contracts where the terms are written directly into code.

Pack your curiosity and skepticism alike as we explore Fintech's complexities and contemplate its vast potential and underlying risks.

Chapter 63: Cryptocurrency
A Real Treasure or Just Digital Fool's Gold?

If you think of money as a way to represent value, then cryptocurrency might be its next evolutionary step in the digital age. A cryptocurrency is a digital or virtual form of currency that uses cryptography to proof and validate transactions instead of commercial banks or other trusted players of the financial industry.

A cryptocurrency is a type of digital or virtual currency that uses cryptography for security. Unlike traditional currencies issued by governments and central banks, cryptocurrencies operate on decentralized technology called blockchain, which is a distributed ledger that records all transactions across a network of computers. Cryptocurrencies exist only in digital form and have no physical counterparts like coins or banknotes. They are represented as digital tokens or coins.

Practical Examples

Bitcoin: Perhaps the most widely recognized cryptocurrency, Bitcoin was the first to leverage blockchain technology, providing a decentralized means for users to exchange value.

Ethereum: Going beyond just a currency, Ethereum allows developers to create decentralized applications on its blockchain.

Dogecoin: Initially started as a meme, Dogecoin has become a legitimate cryptocurrency, showcasing the immense popularity and accessibility of digital currencies.

Potential Pitfalls

Cryptocurrency is not without its challenges. Its decentralized nature, while appealing, also means there's no central authority to govern or stabilize it. Prices can skyrocket, but they can also plummet. Cryptocurrencies are also susceptible to loss if you forget your access keys, and their semi-anonymous nature makes them a popular choice for illicit activities on the internet.

Emerging Trends and Future Outlook

Despite its challenges, the world of cryptocurrency is evolving at a thrilling pace. As decentralized finance (DeFi) platforms gain traction, traditional banks find themselves navigating how to integrate these digital currencies into their existing structures. Moreover, the concept of NFTs (Non-Fungible Tokens) is creating new paradigms for artists, musicians, and content creators to monetize their work in unprecedented ways. While the crypto market oscillates between exciting innovations and notable risks, it undoubtedly paves the way toward a future where finance and technology become ever more intricately entwined.

This glimpse into the intricate world of cryptocurrency hints at not only its potential to reshape our financial landscape but also the need to navigate its waves judiciously. The blend of risk and innovation encapsulates a digital adventure that is uniquely cryptocurrency.

Chapter 64: Bitcoin
What's Hiding Behind the Buzz?

You've likely heard about Bitcoin even if your primary news source is your chatty neighbor. It's everywhere, and it's sparked much debate among financial wizards and many people alike. If money talked, Bitcoin would probably be the buzzword in most of its conversations. But what's behind all the buzz and perplexing jargon?

Bitcoin, introduced by an anonymous entity named Satoshi Nakamoto in 2009, is the first cryptocurrency and is decentralized, meaning no single entity, like a government or central bank, controls it. Transactions are recorded on a public ledger called the blockchain, which is maintained by a network of computers (known as nodes). Its design allows users to send and receive payments, purchase goods, and hold value, all without requiring a middleman, such as a bank or payment provider.

Practical Examples

Investment & Trading: Many individuals and institutional investors buy and hold Bitcoin hoping its value will increase over time. It's been dubbed "digital gold" by some, reflecting its appeal as a store of value.

Purchasing Goods and Services: Some businesses accept Bitcoin as payment. For instance, Overstock.com welcomes Bitcoin for purchases on their platform, from furniture to jewelry.

Potential Pitfalls

As much as Bitcoin has been hailed as a financial revolution, it's not without its troubles. The volatility of its price is legendary, with dramatic price hikes followed by sobering drops. It has also been critiqued for its energy consumption; the process of validating transactions and securing the network, known as mining, consumes an enormous amount of electricity. Furthermore, the regulatory environment is ever-shifting, posing potential risks and benefits to its adoption and valuation.

Emerging Trends and Future Outlook

Bitcoin's journey on the financial rollercoaster has sparked innovations and adaptations in various sectors. While it has fostered the birth of numerous other cryptocurrencies, it has also incited discussions about digital currency adoption at a national level (think CBDCs - Central Bank Digital Currencies). Moreover, Bitcoin is increasingly being eyed by traditional financial institutions as a legitimate asset class, and its underlying technology, blockchain, is finding myriad applications beyond currency, from supply chain management to voting systems. The future of Bitcoin is as tantalizingly uncertain as it is brimming with potential.

The rise of Bitcoin has been nothing short of a financial saga, woven with tales of overnight millionaires and steep, sudden losses. Whether viewed as a high-risk investment, a tool for financial freedom, or a speculative bubble, Bitcoin has indelibly shaped discussions about what we perceive as valuable and trustable. Buckle up, as the journey with Bitcoin and other cryptocurrencies is likely to present even more twists and turns in the future.

Chapter 65: NFT (Non-Fungible Tokens)

A New Digital Renaissance: Owning Pixels, Art, and Moments in Time

Imagine being able to unequivocally prove that you own an exclusive item - say, a digital piece of artwork or a special in-game asset. But wait, we're in the digital realm, where everything is replicable, right? Enter NFTs, where things get delightfully peculiar.

Unlike your typical digital file that can be easily copied and pasted, an NFT is a unique digital asset verified using blockchain technology, ensuring its rarity and authenticity. It's like having a signed, original painting in a digital form. Each NFT has distinct information and attributes that make it stand apart, hence "non-fungible" or not interchangeable on a one-to-one basis.

Practical Examples

Digital Art Auctions: The artwork "Everydays: The First 5000 Days" by artist Beeple was sold for a whopping $69 million as an NFT. Note this was a speculative bubble in 2021 that I hope won't come back.

Virtual Real Estate: People are buying and selling virtual plots in digital spaces in the "metaverse".

Collectible Moments: NBA Top Shot allows fans to buy, sell, and trade officially licensed NBA collectible highlights.

Potential Pitfalls

While the NFT universe is rife with opportunities and has seen a very interesting boom (and burst) in 2021 for art and collectibles, it isn't without its flaws. The environmental impact of minting NFTs, driven by energy-consuming blockchain networks, has been a hot topic of debate. Furthermore, the market is highly speculative, and the perceived value of digital assets can be exceptionally volatile. Plus, issues surrounding copyright and intellectual property in the digital space are still in murky waters, necessitating vigilant navigation. I'm personally not a fan of NFTs and I've been very critical of the 2021 bubble.

Emerging Trends and Future Outlook

The NFT rollercoaster is propelling us into unknown future prospects. Beyond the arts and entertainment sector, NFTs could redefine ownership or traceability and originality in various domains, such as real estate, academia, and more.

Imagine a world where your academic credentials are NFTs, ensuring their authenticity and uniqueness. Moreover, as NFT platforms explore more energy-efficient solutions and additional blockchain networks adopt NFT standards, we might witness a more sustainable, expansive, and inclusive environment for digital assets. Or we might not. Stay tuned and be critical and analytical with the evolution of NFTs.

Chapter 66: Bootstrapping

The Art of Self-Sustained Business Building

Bootstrapping in the business context refers to starting and growing a company without external funding or investment. Instead, entrepreneurs rely on their savings, day-to-day revenues, and personal resources. The term is drawn from the old phrase "pulling oneself up by one's bootstraps," which essentially means improving one's situation through self-initiative.

The bootstrapped approach focuses on profitability from the onset. It requires a keen sense of financial discipline, as entrepreneurs must prioritize essential expenses, make smart decisions based on revenue, and often wear multiple hats to minimize operational costs.

Practical Examples

Mailchimp: This email marketing giant didn't just send newsletters but also sent a message across the entrepreneurial world about bootstrapping's potential. Started in 2001, Mailchimp was diligently built into a billion-dollar business without the influx of external investment.

Basecamp: A project management tool that was not project-managed by external investors. The company was bootstrapped, and it rocketed into success, proving that businesses can scale and be profitable without venturing into the world of venture capital.

Potential Pitfalls

Despite the allure of total control, bootstrapping can tether businesses to numerous challenges. Limited capital might stifle growth or hinder the ability to seize market opportunities swiftly. The financial strain could also lean heavily on the entrepreneurs, where personal and business finances sometimes become inseparably entwined, leading to potential personal financial risk.

Emerging Trends and Future Outlook

The future may witness an amalgamation of bootstrapping and selective investment, where entrepreneurs bootstrap in initial stages and only seek investment when it aligns seamlessly with their strategic vision. The digital era is enabling bootstrapped businesses to employ an array of tools and platforms, such as crowdfunding and online marketplaces, to tap into global markets with minimized costs.

In the tapestry of entrepreneurship, bootstrapping embroiders a pattern of prudence, autonomy, and sometimes, unbridled innovation. It's where every penny is pinched, every strategy is self-weighed, and every success is immensely personal.

Chapter 67: Crowdfunding
Fueling dreams with collective belief.

Imagine inviting a large crowd to your birthday party with a peculiar request: no traditional gifts, but rather a small contribution toward that dreamy gaming console you've been eyeing for months. To your astonishment, the pooled funds from your 100 guests manifest your gaming dreams into reality. This is the essence of crowdfunding, where collective financial contributions make aspirations materialize.

Crowdfunding is a financial practice where entrepreneurs, creators, or anyone with a dream project presents their idea on a platform, inviting people from across the globe to contribute funds. It's not a loan, nor an investment in a traditional sense. It's often a small monetary contribution from a large number of people to support a cause, project, or business they believe in.

Practical Examples

Kickstarter: Perhaps the most widely recognized name in the realm of crowdfunding, Kickstarter has facilitated the fundraising of billions of dollars since its 2009 inception, enabling projects in tech, arts, comics, and an array of other sectors to see the light of day.

Indiegogo: With a global platform that supports contributions through purchases and donations, Indiegogo has paved the way for innovative products and artistic ventures alike, harboring an inclusive environment for a wide variety of projects.

GoFundMe: Steering the ship slightly differently, GoFundMe often hosts campaigns that lean towards personal causes and life events, from medical bills and charitable missions to educational endeavors, offering a supportive platform for individual and community needs.

Potential Pitfalls

Venturing into the world of crowdfunding could mean sailing in occasionally turbulent waters. Risks like falling short of the funding goal, unexpected project hurdles, or managing a sea of backers with varied expectations can pose significant challenges. Moreover, a failed campaign or unmet promises can potentially damage reputation and trust among the crowd.

Emerging Trends and Future Outlook

As we chart into the future, crowdfunding is gradually evolving into a formidable vessel for various ventures, particularly in realms like indie filmmaking, tech innovations, and social enterprises. Emerging trends suggest a potential rise in equity crowdfunding, where backers gain a small equity share, and decentralized finance (DeFi) platforms might redefine crowdfunding landscapes with blockchain technology, ensuring more secure and transparent transactions.

Chapter 68: IPO (Initial Public offering)
The Grand Debut on the Stock Stage

Picture this: a bustling, high-energy party where individuals exchange snippets of paper with fervent excitement, and with each transaction, fortunes rise and dip. This might evoke the imagery of a clandestine gambling den, but we're indeed traversing the vibrant realm of the stock market. Here, the Initial Public Offering (IPO) is akin to an elite party where companies make their stock available to the public for the first time.

An IPO is a pivotal moment in a company's journey, symbolizing its transition from a private to a public entity. By issuing shares to the public, the company opens itself to public investors, aligning its growth and performance with the expectations and prospects of a wider shareholder base. It's a double-edged sword - an influx of capital on one hand, but subjected to the scrutinizing eyes of public stakeholders on the other.

Practical Examples

Alibaba's Gigantic Leap: When the Chinese giant, Alibaba Group, stepped onto the New York Stock Exchange in 2014, it was nothing short of a spectacle. Raising a whopping $25 billion, it currently holds the record for the largest IPO ever, creating a mammoth-sized ripple in the global economic pond.

Facebook's Social Entry: Making headlines in 2012, Facebook's IPO was one of the most anticipated of the tech era. With an initial offering price of $38 per share, it raised $16 billion, marking it as one of the biggest tech IPOs in history.

Snap's Snappy Debut: Snap Inc., the parent company of Snapchat, made a splashy debut in 2017. Priced at $17 per share during its IPO, it witnessed a dramatic 44% jump on its first trading day, epitomizing the fervor that tech companies can generate on the stock market.

Potential Pitfalls

Embarking on an IPO is no casual affair. Companies find themselves subjected to stringent regulations, hefty compliance costs, and a perpetual obligation to appease public shareholders. If the anticipated capital doesn't pour in or if the market reacts unfavorably, the company might stumble upon precarious financial and reputational tightropes.

Emerging Trends and Future Outlook

The horizon forecasts a fascinating panorama of IPO landscapes. With the advent of technologies like blockchain, the emergence of decentralized finance (DeFi) IPO platforms might redefine traditional processes, paving the way for more transparent, secure, and efficient public offerings. Moreover, the burgeoning realm of ESG (Environmental, Social, and Governance) investing is likely to sway IPO strategies, as companies vying for the limelight would need to prance in tandem with sustainable and ethical practices.

Chapter 69: Smart Contract

Scripting the Future of Transactions

Envision entering into an agreement where you're assured that all parties will uphold their end of the bargain, without the need for legal teams or notaries. Your peace of mind emanates not from a signed piece of paper but from lines of code - This is the domain of smart contracts.

A smart contract is a self-executing contract with the terms directly written into code. It operates on a blockchain, ensuring transparency, decentralization, and security. When predetermined conditions are met, the contract automatically triggers the agreed-upon action, be it a financial transaction, release of data, or any predefined outcome.

Practical Examples

Buying Property with a Digital Handshake: Imagine purchasing a property where, upon transferring the agreed cryptocurrency, the digital ownership deed is instantaneously transferred to you, all secured and validated through a smart contract on the blockchain.

Securing Royalties in the Music Industry: Artists could use smart contracts to automatically receive royalties whenever their music is purchased or used, ensuring fair compensation without relying on intermediaries.

Supply Chain Transparency: In logistics, a smart contract can automatically validate and execute transactions when certain conditions are met, like a product reaching its destination, ensuring transparency and efficacy across the supply chain.

Potential Pitfalls

Navigating through smart contracts isn't without its turbulence. The irrevocable nature of these contracts means that once executed, there's no turning back, even if an error is spotted in hindsight. Moreover, their dependence on the blockchain means that if the network is compromised, so too is the trust in the smart contract. Additionally, legal and regulatory frameworks still have catching up to do with this digital innovation, presenting a gray area in dispute resolutions.

Emerging Trends and Future Outlook

Smart contracts pose themselves at the cusp of becoming an integral element in numerous sectors, transcending beyond financial transactions into realms like healthcare, for securing patient data, or in voting systems, for ensuring fair and transparent electoral processes. The ongoing advancements in blockchain technologies and an increasing tilt towards decentralized finance (DeFi) provide a fertile ground for the evolution and adaptation of smart contracts into our digital lives.

As we encode our promises and agreements into the secure and transparent digital ledgers, we weave a future where transactions, big or small, are seamless, direct, and free from the clutches of opaque intermediaries. So, the next time you're venturing into a transaction, a digital contract might just be your secure, invisible ally in the blockchain battleground.

Module 9 Closing

Diving into the diverse and intricate world of finance and fundraising, from the decentralization of assets and financial systems to empowering startups and fostering transparent, automated contractual transactions, it's apparent that financial systems are evolving. These concepts not only operate independently but weave a complex, interlinked, and dynamic tapestry, shaping our contemporary and future financial ecosystems.

We don't know how they will evolve but we know we are in a transformative journey.

Embracing Digital Currency: Cryptocurrency does not merely exist as virtual assets but symbolizes a novel approach toward financial autonomy, decentralization, and globalized transactions in the economic landscape.

Pioneering Decentralized Finance: Bitcoin isn't just a digital currency; it represents a radical shift, pioneering a decentralized approach to finance and challenging conventional monetary systems and controls.

Autonomous Financial Ecosystems: Defi transcends traditional financial boundaries, introducing a framework that enables autonomous, decentralized, and user-centric financial ecosystems, where users exercise greater control and autonomy over their assets -but don't forget- at their risk.

Self-sufficient Startup Journeys: Bootstrapping exemplifies a self-sufficient, resource-optimized approach to startup growth, emphasizing financial prudence and strategically aligned investment in the entrepreneurial journey.

Empowering Innovations through Collective Support: Crowdfunding signifies a democratized approach to financial backing, enabling innovators to harness collective support and empowering communities to directly contribute to bringing ideas to fruition.

Bridging Enterprises and Public Investment: An IPO, or Initial Public Offering , serves not merely as a financial event, but as a pivotal transition, bridging enterprises with the public investment realm and marking a significant milestone in a company's growth journey.

Automated Trust and Transactions: Smart Contracts extend beyond automated agreements, serving as a cornerstone for trustless, automated, and decentralized transactions within the blockchain, revolutionizing conventional contractual mechanisms.

Module 10 - Other Concepts. Last bits and bytes.

Our final module! a bit of digital miscellany, an assortment of concepts that pervade our online experiences yet often elude our awareness. While these notions might initially seem disparate, each contributes indispensably to the intricate tapestry of our digital life.

We are about to dissect the unobtrusive yet vital concept of Backups, delve into the secretive life of Cookies, navigate through the intricate alleys of GDPR, embark on a surreal journey into the Metaverse, and wrap up with the minimalistic beauty of MVP. These seemingly diverse concepts weave a complex web that silently orchestrates much of our digital journey, often unacknowledged yet indispensably vital.

As we delve into this final module, let's get the last bits to complete the mosaic of our digital journey.

Chapter 70: Spam
The Uninvited Digital Guest

Spam, in the context of digital communication, refers to unsolicited messages sent en masse, primarily via email. These messages can be promotional, fraudulent, or even malicious, and are often sent with the intent of reaching as many recipients as possible.

While some spam can be harmless advertisements, others might contain malware, phishing schemes, or scams. With the proliferation of digital platforms, spam has expanded beyond just emails, reaching social media, messaging apps, and more.

Practical Examples

Phishing Scams: Some spam emails impersonate credible entities, such as banks or government organizations, attempting to dupe individuals into revealing personal information. "Verify your account details," they might demand, with a convenient (and deceptive) link attached.

Mass Marketing: Ever received an email boasting of incredible weight-loss secrets, the newest cryptocurrency opportunities, or imploring you to claim a lottery you never entered? That's spam flexing its muscles in mass marketing.

Bot-Generated Comments: Websites and blogs are no strangers to spam, often bombarded with comments like "Great post! Check out [insert random website here] for amazing deals!" Bot-generated spam comments seek to drive unsuspecting traffic to particular websites.

Potential Pitfalls

Spam often masquerades as a benign or even beneficial entity, yet beneath the surface, risks lurk. Falling for a phishing spam email can lead to stolen personal information, financial loss, or unauthorized access to personal accounts. Furthermore, opening attachments or clicking links in spam emails may introduce malware or viruses into your device, jeopardizing data and personal information. For businesses, spam can choke organizational communication channels, reduce productivity, and potentially compromise organizational data.

Emerging Trends and Future Outlook

The future of spam wrestles between evolving to be more sophisticated and being continuously thwarted by advanced spam-filters and cybersecurity measures. With advancements in Artificial Intelligence (AI), spam messages are becoming more adept at mimicking genuine communication, bypassing filters, and effectively reaching inboxes. Conversely, anti-spam technologies are also leveraging AI and Machine Learning (ML) to discern and filter out these unsolicited messages more efficiently. Thus, a tug of war persists between spam strategies becoming more refined and technological advancements creating formidable barriers against them.

Chapter 71: Backup
Your digital safety net

You've spent countless hours laboring over a project, only to have your computer suddenly crash, wiping away all those caffeine-fueled nights and meticulously crafted details. It's the stuff of digital nightmares, right? Fortunately you might have a "Backup,"

A backup is essentially a copy or archive of data that can be used to restore and recover information in the event of data loss. In the digital realm, it's your safety net, catching you when the tightrope of technology snaps unexpectedly.

No matter if it's precious family photos, critical work documents, or a thesis that's been months in the making, having a backup is akin to having a digital insurance policy. It ensures that our data, in all its myriad forms, is not lost to the abyss of accidental deletions, malicious attacks, or hardware failures. It's a precautionary tale that emphasizes a simple message: better safe than sorry.

Practical Examples

Cloud Storage: Utilizing platforms like Google Drive or Dropbox, individuals and businesses alike store copies of their essential data online. This allows for easy retrieval even if their physical devices malfunction or data is otherwise lost.

External Hard Drives: Many choose to store a copy of their essential data on external hard drives. In the event that their computer gives up the ghost, their data remains safe and accessible on an external device.

Server Backups: In an organizational context, regular backups of servers ensure that customer data, transaction histories, and other pivotal data are not lost amid technical issues, thus safeguarding both operations and reputation.

Potential Pitfalls

Navigating through the landscape of backups may seem straightforward, but perils lurk in the shadows. The potential risk of choosing unreliable backup platforms, neglecting regular backup updates, or failing to secure backup data from potential cyber threats can reverse the very purpose of backups. Also, partial backups or backup failures may mean that not all data is retrievable when calamity strikes. Thus, ensuring a robust, secure, and consistent backup strategy is pivotal.

Emerging Trends and Future Outlook

The future of backups looks secure, intelligent, and more automated. With the advent of smarter technologies, backup systems are evolving to become more intuitive, automatically updating, and integrating more seamlessly with our daily digital activities. Moreover, as the cloud becomes more secure and robust, cloud backups will likely proliferate, offering more space, more security, and facilitating easy access to data, anywhere, anytime. The conversation around backups will also likely intertwine with discussions about data security, given the sensitive nature of information often stored.

Chapter 72: Cookies
Your Digital Trail

Remember when browsing an online store, leaving, and then seeing ads for it everywhere you virtually go. It's like your digital shopping cart became a boomerang, constantly returning to you. That's digital cookies at work, trailing your online steps, understanding your preferences, and sometimes, tossing tailored ads your way.

Digital cookies are tiny files that websites store on your device. They remember your actions and preferences (like login, language, and other settings) and recognize you and your device upon return to the site. It's like a digital footprint that allows websites to understand user behavior and provide a personalized browsing experience, enabling websites to remember you, just as your favorite barista remembers your daily brew.

Practical Examples

Online Shopping: Ever put something in a shopping cart and come back later to find it still there? Thank cookies for that convenient memory.

Language Preferences: If you visit a global website and choose your preferred language, cookies ensure that you'll see the site in that language on your next visit.

Ad Targeting: You search for a pair of shoes, and suddenly, ads for similar footwear seem to be everywhere? Third-party cookies are tracking your preferences to serve relevant ads.

Potential Pitfalls

Cookies, while useful, have stirred up a fair bit of controversy, particularly concerning privacy. The ubiquitous "Accept Cookies?" pop-ups stem from regulations intending to protect user data, as cookies can be used to compile long-term records of individuals' browsing histories. For users, it's crucial to understand which cookies a website uses and how your data will be utilized and protected. Additionally, overly aggressive cookie tracking may hinder user experience and deter visitors.

Emerging Trends and Future Outlook

In a world increasingly concerned with data privacy, cookies are in the spotlight. The future is likely to see a shift towards more transparent practices regarding cookie usage and data handling, ensuring that user privacy is respected. Enhanced cookie management tools and increasing user control over personal data are emerging trends, with more browsers offering rigorous cookie blocking features. It's a delicate balance, ensuring user privacy while delivering tailored experiences, which is likely to define the digital cookie journey in times ahead.

Chapter 73: GDPR
Navigating the Seas of Data Protection

The General Data Protection Regulation, or GDPR, isn't some arcane spell from a fantasy novel. It's a critical piece of legislation implemented by the European Union (EU) in 2018, designed to ensure the protection and privacy of individuals' personal data.

In a nutshell, GDPR mandates how businesses can collect, store, and use personal data of EU citizens. It emphasizes user consent, data transparency, and the right to be forgotten (meaning users can request their data be deleted). Non-compliance? It can result in hefty fines, sometimes running into millions.

Practical Examples

Right to be Forgotten: If you've ever requested to have your account and associated data deleted from a platform (like asking a virtual captain to throw your past purchases overboard), that's the GDPR at work, ensuring your right to be forgotten.

Data Breach Notifications: Should a digital storm (data breach) compromise your ship (data), companies under GDPR are required to notify you within 72 hours of becoming aware of the breach, ensuring you can take protective action.

Data Access Requests: Ever wanted to know what data a company holds on you? Under GDPR, you can request an organization to share the personal data they've stored about you.

Potential Pitfalls

Navigating through the GDPR isn't always smooth sailing. For businesses, compliance can be intricate and resource-intensive, requiring a meticulous understanding of data handling and protection processes. Additionally, the global nature of the digital world makes navigating GDPR compliance complex for organizations operating internationally, as they must steer through varying data protection regulations in different regions.

Emerging Trends and Future Outlook

As the digital world evolves, expect to see a surge in similar data protection regulations cropping up across different continents. Enhanced focus on ensuring businesses treat data ethically and transparently will shape the future of digital interactions. Innovations will likely steer towards developing tools and frameworks to aid organizations in maintaining compliance while ensuring seamless user experiences.

Chapter 74: The Metaverse
Your Passport to Infinite Digital Universes

Remember when the idea of living in a digital universe was limited to sci-fi films? Well, we might be there already.

The Metaverse refers to a collective, virtual shared space that is created by the convergence of physical and virtual reality. This space isn't limited to a single virtual world; it encompasses the entirety of digital space created by all connected virtual and augmented reality (VR/AR) platforms. Here, you can interact with a computer-generated environment and other users in real-time. It's like stepping into a sci-fi movie where you can hop between different realities, experiencing each uniquely, all without ever needing to leave your room.

Practical Examples

Socializing in Virtual Reality: Platforms like VRChat and Facebook's Horizon Workrooms enable users to socialize and collaborate in a virtual space, employing avatars and VR technology to immerse themselves in a digital environment.

Gaming: In games like Fortnite and Roblox, players from around the world engage not only in gameplay but also in social activities, collaborative projects, and even attend concerts, reflecting a nascent metaverse experience.

Virtual Shopping: Imagine trying on clothes, walking through digital malls, or designing your dream home in a virtual world. Projects like Decentraland are pioneering this, enabling users to buy, develop, and sell parcels of virtual real estate.

Potential Pitfalls

The road to the metaverse is filled with challenges and quandaries. Questions about data privacy, economic inequality, and digital ownership loom large. A truly inclusive metaverse must address digital divides and ensure access to all, to avoid creating parallel universes where only certain individuals can participate, while others are left behind.

Emerging Trends and Future Outlook

In the sprawling realms of the metaverse, the boundaries between reality and virtuality blur. Expect to see an upsurge in decentralized platforms, where users have control over their digital assets and experiences. Moreover, innovations in VR/AR technology, blockchain, and artificial intelligence will propel us further into a future where our digital and physical worlds become inseparably intertwined.

Chapter 75: MVP (Minimum Viable Product)

Crafting the Bare Minimum Yet Impactful Products

You have a brilliant idea for a product, but is the world ready for it? Before investing countless resources, smart innovators turn to MVPs. An MVP, or Minimum Viable Product, is a version of a new product that allows a team to collect the maximum amount of validated learning about customers with the least effort.

It's not about creating a half-baked or 'unfinished' product. Instead, it's about focusing on core features to meet primary objectives and getting it to the market to test its viability. In essence, an MVP helps determine the product's potential success without fully committing.

Practical Examples

Dropbox: Before becoming the popular cloud storage platform it is today, Dropbox started as a simple MVP. A video demonstrating its functioning was released, creating a massive user waitlist overnight. The response validated the market need, propelling its further development.

Airbnb: Started with a simple site to rent out space during conferences. Now, it's a global platform for accommodation and experiences.

Zappos: Before establishing a full-blown online store, the founder posted photos of shoes online to gauge interest and bought them from stores only when someone placed an order.

Potential Pitfalls

Launching an MVP is not without challenges. Misjudging the "minimum" can lead to underdeveloped products that fail to showcase value, whereas misinterpreting "viable" may cause overshooting resources. Striking a balance, wherein the product displays enough functionality and appeal to entice early adopters while safeguarding resources, is vital.

Emerging Trends and Future Outlook

In the era where lean startups are the norm, MVPs will persist as a smart strategy to validate business ideas without excessive risk. Technologies like AI and IoT will play pivotal roles in MVP development, enabling creators to develop smarter, more connected, and more adaptable products with minimal builds.

MVP is your telescope to peer into the future prospects of your product, allowing you to navigate through the cosmic ocean of market trends and consumer behaviors with minimized risks and optimized efforts.

Module 10 Closing.

What a ride! As we finished the last module, these concepts not only stand alone in their individual capacities but are intertwined. Let's recap them:

Navigating through Digital Clutter: Spam Exemplifies the complexities and nuisances within our digital communication channels, necessitating advanced filtering and safeguard mechanisms to ensure communicative efficiency and security.

Guardianship of Digital Assets: The practice of creating Backups transcends mere data preservation, embodying a proactive approach toward safeguarding digital assets.

Balancing Personalization and Privacy: Cookies straddle the delicate balance between personalized user experiences and intrinsic privacy concerns, urging for a judicious application in our interconnected digital landscapes.

Upholding User Sovereignty: GDPR isn't just regulation but a statement, underscoring the criticality of user privacy and control, fortifying the user's sovereignty over their digital footprints in the virtual domain.

Exploring Virtual Horizons: The Metaverse unfurls not merely as a virtual space but as an expansive new universe, offering boundless possibilities and redefining interactions, transactions, and experiential realities in the digital realm.

Pragmatic Approach to Solution Crafting: MVP or Minimum Viable Product manifests as a pragmatic methodology in solution crafting, prioritizing core functionalities and value propositions, ensuring agile, user-centric, and feedback-driven product development.

Afterword

If the journey through this book has shown anything beyond the bytes and bits, it's the revelation that the digital landscape is continuously evolving. While I hope reading it has helped you improve and reinforce your tech foundations, your journey should not finish here.

As you process the knowledge from these pages, remember, this is just a single station in the never ending technology evolution.

By now you should have a good foundation around tech concepts and I invite you from now on to welcome the unknown with open arms and a curious mind. Engage in with friends and co-workers, join discussions, enroll in courses, and never shy away from a new app, platform, or tool.

Remember, each of you is a digital pioneer. Your unique experiences, insights, and applications will contribute to this collective digital society we're all building that should be as inclusive as possible.

I hope you use your new knowledge to help build and create a better world for our children, explore new passions and hobbies, and always, always remain curious.

I really appreciate you've made it till here and your eagerness to go through the difficult depths of digital technology. Your personal commitment to update yourself is very inspiring and says a lot about you.

I'm feeling very lucky to have had your attention and I hope you've enjoyed this journey. May our paths cross again in new editions and other themes over coming years.

I also want to thank my siblings and close friends for all the advice and feedback they gave me during this creation process and my father, who made me a curious and creative mind.

Thank you.

Jordi.

Every time something comes to an end,
something else begins.

What are you going to do next?